RIATA RANCH
COWBOY GIRLS

RIATA RANCH
COWBOY GIRLS

Life Lessons Learned on the Back of a Horse

Tom Maier with Rebekah Ferran Witter

Photography by William Shepley

Foreword by Larry Mahan

STOREY
BOOKS

The mission of Storey Communications is to serve our customers by publishing practical information that encourages personal independence in harmony with the environment.

The Riata Ranch Cowboy Girls are highly skilled riders who have been practicing their routines for years under the guidance of expert coaches. Their horses are highly trained, familiar with trick-riding routines, and proven to be reliable. Safety is always part of Riata Ranch activities, and the Cowboy Girls use only equipment that is specifically designed for trick-riding. The publisher strongly cautions readers not to attempt any of these trick-riding routines, even the simplest-looking, without step-by-step training with a qualified instructor. Safety helmets are recommended for all riders, especially beginners.

Editorial Director, Storey Books: Margaret J. Lydic
Edited by Deborah Burns
Art direction by Meredith Maker
Photographs by William Shepley, with the following exceptions, which are courtesy of Riata Ranch: pages viii, 2, 3, 4, 5, 6 (bottom), 7, 8, 9, 10, 11, 12, 13, 15, 16, 17, 18 (top), 22 (left), 43, 70, 71 (left), 79, 82, 90, 130, 133, and 138.
Cover and interior design by Carol Jessop, Black Trout Design; and Meredith Maker
Text production by Susan Bernier

Printed in Hong Kong by C & C Offset Printing Co. Ltd.

10 9 8 7 6 5 4 3 2 1

Library of Congress Cataloging-in-Publication Data

Maier, Tom, 1928-
    Riata Ranch Cowboy Girls: life lessons learned on the back of a horse / Tom Maier with Rebekah Ferran Witter ; photographs by William Shepley ; foreword by Larry Mahan.
        p. cm.
    ISBN 1-58017-365-9 (alk. paper)
    1. Riata Ranch (California) 2. Riata Ranch Cowboy Girls.
3. Horsemanship 4. Trick riding. 5. Show riding. I. Witter, Rebekah Ferran. II. Title.
SF310.C22 R536 2001
798.2'3—dc21
                                                                    00-069852

It's showtime for Kansas Carradine

Contents

FOREWORD

Riata Ranch is a magical place where young people can realize their own personal dreams and goals. The visionary who created it, basing it on his own personal history and life experiences, is Tom Maier. His vision has been to educate, communicate with, and motivate young people, and his goal is to develop the whole person, physically, mentally, emotionally, and spiritually.

From the bottom up, Riata Ranch has a plan for each and every aspect of the program, devised with creativity, flexibility, and imagination. The students do all of the work on the ranch. In this setting they learn discipline, respect, history, self-confidence, athleticism, and showmanship and develop a lasting relationship with one of the most magnificent animals in the world, the horse.

Tom has created a mind / body experience that changes people's thoughts, attitudes, and actions and helps them move toward a higher level of being. The program is extremely physical, of course, which keeps everyone in great shape. The choreography and artistry are mentally tough and demanding, and the camaraderie and sportsmanship are the glue that holds it all together.

The entire ranch is run on the Zen principle of mindfulness: When you rake, rake; when you feed, feed. Do only one thing at a time, and become what you do. Let your mind transcend your body, and live by pure awareness in each and every moment. No talking, no distractions; just mindfulness! From this principle, amazing things can

happen. A new sense of self develops, and daily rituals take on a life of their own.

What impresses me most is that Tom has brought together all the working ingredients that build human character. He demands that each student learn and respect the daily rituals of the horse and the ranch, and he provides a phenomenal mentoring program.

Each Riata parent is proud to say, "That's my daughter!" because she is experiencing a unique education. It's an education in positive human development, where the core of one's essence is more important than the end result.

I cannot even begin to tell you how impressed I am with the vision of Tom Maier, the mission of Riata Ranch, and the Riata Ranch Cowboy Girls!

Let the show begin!

Larry Mahan
Six-time World Champion Cowboy,
Professional Rodeo Cowboys
Association

PREFACE

At an early age I left my home and family in North Dakota and landed in California. There I fell into the hands of men who represented the last of a breed. These men became mentors and the grandfathers I never knew. Their values were based on common sense and a proud lifestyle dictated by nature. The philosophy of Riata Ranch is a combination of the values of these men: Gene Holder, Mickey Milrick, Ky Wilhoit, W. V. Smith, Carl Ward, Adolf Gill, Clay Carr, Gene Rambo, J. Ralph Bell, Lou Kosloff, and Jonny Mendes.

After doubling for women in movies, riding sale horses at the L.A. Horse & Mule outfit, working day jobs for the Gill Cattle Company, riding good horses, and going into the cattle business for myself, I finally got the chance to become a professional rodeo cowboy as a calf roper. But my dream of a rodeo career was cut short by an automobile accident, and in 1957 I started Riata Ranch. Now it was my turn to pass on the values, common sense, and way of life that was becoming a distant memory in modern life. It became my passion to teach young people the life lessons that had been passed on to me by my mentors. During its first 20 years, Riata Ranch attracted many distinguished people who were drawn to the concept of young people learning life skills built on the Code of the West. Howard Way, Chief Arnold Rojas, Felix Guitron, Barbara Worth, Wilma Tate, Clorie Gill, and my very special friend, Greg Ward, all contributed to the Riata philosophy. I became keenly aware that the people who were attracted to Riata Ranch were those who were the best in their field and the real thing.

Working with young people has opened many doors and enlightened me far beyond what I ever imagined. When we started traveling and performing, the performance team was made up of four 13-year-old girls, and I had no idea or intention of making Riata Ranch an international organization. Today, I am fortified by those who recognize the value in the Riata program and have a desire to see the values taught at Riata Ranch become significant again. The Riata Ranch Cowboy Girls could not have reached the acclaim they have without the support of Bob Tallman, Cotton Rosser, Bob Cook, Jack Roddy, Montie Montana, Nancy Bragg, Larry Mahan, Randy Corley, Bob Fiest, Shawn Davis, Edith Happy, Leon & Vickie Adams, Glenn Randell, Francisco Zamora, Will Rogers Jr., Jimmie Rogers, Gene McLaughlin, Rex Rossi, and J. W. Stoker. Today Riata Ranch enjoys acclaim around the world, thanks to people such as Horst Geier, Jack VanCowenberg, Antonio Aguilar, and my true friend, the late Wolf Krober.

We couldn't do what we do at Riata Ranch without safety measures built into every step of our program. These have been fine-tuned over many years and include training, fitness, tack care, and understanding the nature of horses.

But none of this could have happened without the Riata Ranch parents who entrusted me with their children. It is the Riata parents to whom I dedicate this book. They were and are my greatest supporters in the goals and dreams I created for their children. Riata Ranch has become a tapestry of the mentors in my life, the inspiration from some of the best in the business, and the indisputable support of many parents over nearly five decades of Riata Ranch. To them I very humbly say thank you for allowing me to be a part of the most precious thing you have, your children.

Tom Maier
Riata Ranch International

Left: The Riata Ranch branding iron. Right: Tom Maier poses with (standing) Elizabeth Beltran, Idalia Reveles, and Paula Herrera, and (seated) Kansas Carradine, Cynthia Beltran, and Jennifer Welch.

The Road to Riata

Spectacular is the only word to describe a performance by the Riata Ranch Cowboy Girls. They streak into the arena on their Appaloosa horses, vaulting on and off at a full gallop, hanging just above the horse's flying hooves, standing tall and brandishing American flags, their faces glowing with excitement. These young California women and girls have dazzled audiences around the world with their daring trick-riding routines.

But for Riata Ranch team members the performance is just the glittering tip of the iceberg. These aren't just flashy cowgirls; these girls are *hands* in the best Western tradition. They can ride, rope, show, and beat the toughest competition. They are girls, but they are also crackerjack cowboys.

Tom Maier, founder of Riata Ranch, knows what it takes to be a real cowboy. He has spent a lifetime living and sharing that proud tradition. Tom was born in 1928 of stoic German stock in Sutton, Nebraska. As the eldest of five in a hardscrabble farming family during the Great Depression Tom quickly learned that life — survival — depended on hard work, sharp wits, and sheer determination.

The Riata Ranch Cowboy Girls proudly wear their team jackets in 1984. The troupe's founder, Tom Maier, calls the girls "a rare combination of audacity and innocence."

Prairie Roots

When his family moved to Jamestown, North Dakota, six-year-old Tom was put in charge of driving and caring for teams of horses operating huge mowing, cultivating, and grain-binding machines. Despite his tender age, Tom proved so capable that neighbors often called on him to help with their fieldwork. This led Tom to invent his fantasy hero, "Sundown Tom," a mystery person who always saved the day for those in need but was seen only as he and his spirited steed rode off into the sunset.

In that harsh territory, even elementary school was a trial. Classes were held in an abandoned railroad car. Seven-year-old Tom spoke no English, just German, and his teacher hadn't yet graduated from high school. But she read Will James's book *Smokey* to her students, and from that day forward Tom wanted to be a cowboy.

Hollywood Detour

By 1941 the Depression had claimed their farm and the Maiers fell on desperate times. So, in the dead of winter, twelve-year-old Tom and an eighteen-year-old neighbor, Gene Holder, left home in search of work. Tom was under the impression they were headed for cattle country in Arizona, but Gene told him he had to "stop off" in Los Angeles first. Lacking a grasp of geography, Tom simply shrugged and followed the older boy's lead. The boys were astounded by the lavish lifestyle they saw in Los Angeles. Their planned stop turned into a lifelong sojourn in southern California.

Tom's Life in the Movies

With the Second World War on, jobs and opportunities were plentiful. Gene established the company Movieland Animals, quickly achieving fame as a supplier of wild and exotic beasts for entertainments around the world.

Tom, meanwhile, was employed first by a renowned drill team, Victor McLaughlin's "Light Horse Troupe," and was then hired by Dubrock's, the world's largest riding academy. At Dubrock's Tom fell under the tutelage of stunt coordinator Mickey Millrick. There he performed the daring feat still featured today at the Gene Autry Western Heritage Museum in a film clip from *Ali Baba and the Forty Thieves:* jumping a horse 30 feet, ledge to ledge, over a chasm 300 feet deep. Soon Tom was working with such Hollywood greats as Ronald Reagan in *Stallion Road* and doubling for Elizabeth Taylor in *National Velvet,* Betty Hutton in *Perils of Pauline,* and Jennifer Jones in *Duel in the Sun.*

Tom Maier donned a wig to double for Jennifer Jones in the 1946 motion picture Duel in the Sun. *This publicity shot was taken at the Horse Palace on Riverside Drive in Los Angeles, California.*

During this time Tom lived on a San Fernando Valley ranch owned by Ky Wilhoit, who later became wrangler for the television series *Rawhide,* which launched Clint Eastwood's career. Through Ky, Tom met many of the greatest cowboys and rodeo contestants of the era: Shorty Valdez, Vern Castro, Ben Johnson, Clay Carr, and Eddie Yanez. These renowned hands taught Tom cowboy skills and true Western values.

Although movie work was exciting, Tom still longed to be a "real Will James kind of cowboy," so he left stunt work in Hollywood for ranch work in California's vast San Joaquin Valley. Originally hired to train horses for Bill Smith, a prominent rancher in Exeter, Tom also signed on for day jobs with the fabled Gill Cattle Company, where he honed his cowboy skills. A natural with a rope, Tom could lasso a hundred calves a day. His talent soon became his passion, and Tom soaked up every roping technique he saw.

Down the "Rodeo Road"

About the time Tom fell in love with throwing a loop, he was thrown for a loop by falling in love with Ethelene "Vickie" Vickers. After a few years' courtship, they married and leased a 5000-acre ranch in Badger, California, where Tom ran a cow-calf operation. With the

> **"In rodeo, Tom found what he truly wanted to do. His zeal and passion fortified his commitment. There was no other interest in his life, and he worked hard."**
>
> — Jennifer Welch
> **Manager, Riata Ranch**

Top: Tom Maier with his son Clay Exeter in the 1950s. Clay was named after Clay Carr, the "Babe Ruth" of rodeo cowboys and one of Tom's mentors. *Bottom:* Today Clay is an accomplished horseman who owns and trains Friesan horses.

happy arrival of sons, Clay and Burrel, life was splendid — until the bottom fell out of the beef market and Tom was forced to find another source of income. Deciding to bet on his passion, Tom headed down "Rodeo Road" in search of fame and fortune.

Thankfully, that year (1956) Lady Luck joined Tom on that tough road: He had natural talent, a good horse, a positive attitude, and a championship year. Big wins at Palm Springs and the California Rodeo in Salinas bolstered his professional status. But then, at Salinas, Lady Luck gave up her seat beside Tom to a rodeo buddy who needed a ride home. Grateful for the lift, Tom's buddy volunteered for the first driving shift so Tom could relax.

The sudden grab of brakes woke Tom. Then the scream of twisting metal filled the air as the horse trailer was catapulted on top of the car. Miraculously, Tom survived; the only thing that died in the wreck was his dream of fame and fortune. A crushed knee killed his rodeo career and threw him into dire financial straits.

Starting a Riding School

Hearing of Tom's plight, Robert Hayden, the local district attorney, called to ask whether Tom would teach his son to ride. Although Tom loved riding, he had no experience or interest in teaching children about horses. However, with winter coming, a young family to support, and a physical handicap, he was in no position to decline. Desperation forced him to take the job.

Word of the new riding school spread like quicksilver, and Tom soon had eleven paying students. Desperation may have forced him into teaching, but now dedication pushed him on to create lesson plans. Using an ancient (1938) United States Cavalry manual, Tom stayed a chapter ahead of his students in learning all about equestrian equipment, maneuvers, and nomenclature.

RIATA RANCH

Shortly after the school began, Tom's landlord sold his property and the Maiers had to move once again. This time Tom borrowed a down payment and purchased six acres of scrub with a small house on it at the end of Avenue 300 on the far side of the tracks. With characteristic energy and enthusiasm, Tom cleared the land and began developing his newest dream: Riata Ranch, a place like no other, where young people would learn horsemanship, Western values, cowboy skills, rodeo thrills, and much, much more.

Riata is the Spanish word for rope, and indeed the cowboy rope has been the golden thread woven through Tom's life. He made his students — both boys and girls at first — into topnotch cowboys, and they roped, rode, learned about horses, and eventually competed in rodeos and horse shows throughout Southern California. Along the way, they learned who they were, where they were going, and what they would need to get there.

Developing a "Do Your Best" Attitude

After that first winter of 1957, enrollment exploded to fifty-four youngsters from all over the area. Tom continued expanding and refining the curriculum with classes and

For $12 a month, the original Riata students learned lessons in horsemanship and in living.

tests covering seven levels of ability in Western, English, and rodeo disciplines. Every month, along with the tuition bill of $12, test papers were sent home so parents could track their child's progress. A point system was set up to record ability in chores, tests, and competitions, with the high-point winner being named Riata Ranch All-Around Champion at year's end.

The real price of admission for Riata students was clearly understood: They had to toe the line and give their all. Tom is demanding, and excuses don't cut it. At Riata you're expected to do your best and *be* your best because every job counts and every action is noticed. No one wants to let Tom down, for they know in their hearts they belong at Riata Ranch and they want to stay.

The Best Place in the World

"At Riata everything revolved around the horses, but what really happened was we became a family; all the students became our brothers and sisters," says Brenda [Caskey] Sampietro, one of Tom's first students. "And it was the best place in the world for youngsters because we were always active. We'd rush out as early as we could and stay as long as Tommy would allow — until dark — working, riding, cleaning stalls, raking. We did anything just to be out there. At Riata, there was always something going on."

Another Riata rider who went on to become a professional equestrian trainer, Liz Malloch Doe, adds, "The hardest part of Riata

Top: *The ranch sign shows the Riata Rafter-Double R brand.* **Bottom:** *In 1957, seven-year-old Suzy Cooper (shown with Tom Maier) won the "name-the-ranch" contest. Riata is the Spanish word for rope.*

wasn't the high standards or demanding challenges. Those were tough, but the hardest part was having to leave at the end of the day. We never wanted to leave the magic of Riata."

A Feeling of Belonging

"Riata was important to us because we were important at Riata," concurs Laurie McWilliams, one of the original trick-riding team members. "At Riata, everyone felt like she *belonged*. We were part of something *big* . . . bigger than we'd ever dared dream on our own before. It seemed bigger than family."

Perhaps it seemed bigger than family because the Riata spirit infected so many family members. With their children so excited, parents quickly got caught up in the fervor of Riata themselves. Through the Riata Ranch Parents' Association, whole families would gather for work details, to lend support to horse show teams, or to help with special events. At one point, a parents' brigade moved an old gas station building onto the ranch and transformed it into a party house and rehearsal hall that became known as the Wrangler Room. Riata's "can-do spirit" proved as contagious within families as measles, only lots more fun!

RIATA FANTASYLAND

The dusty, quiet farming community of Exeter had never seen anything like Riata Ranch. Tom's non-stop imagination and Hollywood connections turned Riata into an adventureland to rival anything Walt Disney could conjure up. There were the horses, the

roping, the round-ups, play days with rescue races, goat-tying, and musical tires; there were river runs, wild animals, and long rides to places with names like Buck Rock, Shady Acres, Big Meadows, Suicide Hill.

Everything was so exciting and challenging that Riata students literally jumped out of bed at daybreak to get to the Ranch as early as possible for the day's adventure, whatever that might be. You just never knew what Tom had in mind because most minds couldn't conceive of the outrageous fun Tom served up on a daily basis. Tom always said, "If you're going to be around horses . . . enjoy them." And enjoy them they did!

Tom Maier and Carrie Sue Gill participate with Sierra Bingo in a rescue race. In this drill, the student has to stand with trust as Tom gallops toward her, turns around her as in a stake race, and picks her up onto his saddle. Tom developed this test of trust, confidence, and ability from his work in the movies.

"I never saw such good hands. They could rope, cut, herd cows. Tom stretched them. These girls were doing things that girls traditionally couldn't do."

— Larry Reynolds
Cowboy and Riata parent

For starters, when the relentless valley sun sucked the life out of everyone until their tails were dragging, Tom would treat them to taildraggin' in the nearby Kaweah river. Racing bareback in chest-deep water each rider would slide off the horse, grab his tail, and get dragged behind — one exhilarating way to beat the heat!

Other days everyone would gather at the oak-studded park known as Sleepy Hollow for a free-wheeling game of cops and robbers on horseback. Then there were cattle drives and camp-outs, with songs around the fire. Weekends were filled with rodeo and cutting competitions, gymkhanas and horse shows.

As if all that weren't enough excitement to thrill a kid, Tom and his old friend Gene Holder traded wild and exotic animals back and forth like kids trading baseball cards. Before you could say, "They're off," the Riata Ranch regulars were featured as wild animal jockeys for opening day at Hollywood Park, racing an unruly menagerie of camels, elephants, zebras, longhorn steers, buffaloes, ostriches, and even a hippopotamus around the track!

"It was my distinct pleasure to ride the hippopotamus," laughs Granger Glenn. "Ohhh, *nasty!* They say hippos 'sweat blood.' . . . They don't, it just *looks* like blood. It's some red slime that oozes all over their skin. It was impossible to hang on to that thing!"

Hippo racing, now there's an activity few families consider!

Opposite: *Tom Maier's son Burrel Rambo Maier holds the lines as a ranger at Wawona Living History Center, Yosemite National Park. Burrel, named after rodeo champion Gene Rambo, acquired his cowboy skills as he grew up on the ranch.*

Halloween Blast

If "normal" days were fun at Riata, holidays were the best. Halloween became a theatrical production with ghoulish dramas played out in the moonlit woods of Sleepy Hollow. Mounted performers wore authentic movie costumes, courtesy of Tom's Hollywood cohorts: a full gorilla suit; the original Mummy's outfit and, appropriately, the Headless Horseman. Needless to say, the effect was stunning and scared the wits out of the young audience seated in the hay wagon. At one point, as the wagon rolled past, the ancient, tattered mummy rose from a shallow grave to menace little ones on board. Hysteria prevailed.

The most remarkable episode took place on a moonless Halloween night in 1959 when the script called for the Headless Horseman to face Zorro. Down the trail the Headless Horseman raced with his cape flying and a

Above and below: In addition to riding horses, Riata students rode a range of exotic animals, including llamas, camels, and elephants.

glowing, evil-looking jack-o-lantern tucked in the crook of his arm. Suddenly, from behind a tree Zorro rode out, ordering the Horseman to stop. The Horseman merely laughed derisively, so Zorro raised his sword in threat.

At that dramatic moment, with Zorro's sword raised on high, the eastern sky erupted in brilliant light, filling the heavens and Sleepy Hollow with an explosive, unearthly radiance. Everyone was astounded by the spectacular special effects Tom had arranged. All soon realized, however, that this sensational staging was not Tom's genius at work, but rather an atomic test blast in the Nevada desert!

Storming down Suicide Hill

During the Christmas season there was always a ride for advanced students to Rocky Hill. This annual trek turned legendary one winter when a weather pattern called the Siberian Express blew through, flash-freezing the valley air. The riders headed out in the early morning frost and fog for the four-hour ride to the top of Rocky Hill, where they'd enjoy a Christmas picnic. "That year we were running behind," notes Granger Glenn, "so, on the way back, Tom asked the Double A riders to take a shortcut down the steep side of the Hill.

"Now, that thing was *steep*. You'd take one step off the side and slide four steps down, with your horse's tail up so high it's hittin' your head! But the Double A's were hellacious

Top: *Laurie McWilliams and Kathy Copley cross a river during a Saturday adventure at Riata Ranch.*
Bottom: *Kathy Copley works a steer at the ranch.*

riders and they just went hell-bound-for-election off the side of that mountain. They cut their horses loose and flew over the edge like the scene in *Man from Snowy River!*" From then on, "Suicide Hill" became a rite of passage and badge of courage for daring Riata riders.

Summer Magic at Bass Lake

Another unforgettable chapter in Riata history was written during the summers of 1963 to 1966 when Tom moved the entire operation to a rustic mountain ranch at Bass Lake, near Yosemite, to escape the worst of the valley heat. Here Riata students continued competitive horsemanship training and also ran a string of rental horses for tourists and the neighboring camp, Santa Teresita. Tom assigned his young charges adult responsibilities: Sixteen-year-olds David Manchester and Richard Harris were wranglers in charge of twenty head of horses, and Granger Glenn was named maintenance manager. Older kids were in charge of younger ones, becoming big-brother or big-sister mentors passing on Riata routines, skills, and values.

A Moment to Remember

While responsibilities at Bass Lake expanded, living quarters shrank. There was only a single cabin to house Tom, his wife Vickie, and all the girls, so the boys were housed in the barn's hayloft. The hard work, close quarters, idyllic environment, and daily adventures combined to create, if not a life-

With a little bit of help, all Riata students are capable of mounting any size horse with style. Mounting, both with a saddle and bareback, is a Riata trademark at horse shows.

altering experience, certainly a life-strengthening one for all involved.

"Once at Bass Lake, when the moon was coming up especially bright and beautiful, Tommy made a campfire and we sat around sharing stories and memories," recalls Brenda Sampietro. "All of a sudden, the strains of 'Ghost Riders in the Sky' welled up, and as we raised our eyes from the fire, we saw through the shimmering heat a ridgeline of Indians with headdresses, on Paint ponies silhouetted against the evening sky. Tom had had the boys dress up and appear for us. I'll never forget that. . . . I was thirteen, and it was magic."

"We loved, we laughed, we danced with the horses of Riata, and we all came away better for having been lucky enough to be part of that legacy."

— Liz Malloch Doe,
Riata alumna

Getting Their Acts Together

Such magical experiences and the many thrilling show venues made Tom realize that Riata Ranch isn't a place: It's an attitude of respect and discipline that's ingrained in all who learn to live by the Riata brand.

Riata girl Chris Vincent won the title of Miss Rodeo America in 1970. As the winner in a nationwide competition, she served as a spokesperson for professional rodeo.

Throughout the sixties and seventies Riata continued honing its horse show "Special Classes" until, by 1975, Riata Ranch was recognized as one of the most complete equestrian schools in the United States, with nearly one hundred regular students enrolled in five levels of riding. By instilling the values of purposeful practice, organized preparation, and proper presentation in its students Riata established its competitive reputation and reaped the rewards. Riata students won regional, state, and national championships in Western, English, and Junior Rodeo disciplines as well as twenty-nine Rodeo Queen titles, including Miss Rodeo America!

Developing Life Skills

More important, these same principles gave Riata regulars vital tools with which to become winners in whatever arena they chose to enter in life. Riata alums have moved on to success in such highly competitive fields as rodeo and equestrian sports, medicine, modeling, acting, law, business, television communication, and theatrical production.

Now a successful trainer, Riata alum Liz Malloch Doe writes, "My life is my own now and horses have been with me every step of the way. I owe a lot of that to Tom and Riata. I will forever remain grateful for the personal architecture and torch that is Riata."

This publicity photo from the early 1980s shows (left to right) Kathy Copley, Robin Long, Laurie McWilliams, Lillis Lancaster, Margie Brackett, Kim Parker, Julie Negard, Jennifer Welch, Sharon Lewis, and Janna Copley.

The four original members of the Riata Ranch trick-riding team made their professional debut in 1976 at the Buck Owens Rodeo in Bakersfield, California. From left to right on horseback are Janna Copley, Jennifer Welch, Laurie McWilliams, and Lori "PeeWee" Moreno, all 14 years old. Also making his professional debut was young Bob Tallman (center), who has since been honored, many times, by the Professional Rodeo Cowboys Association as Announcer of the Year.

Kansas Carradine

(Cowboy Girl from 1990 to present)

"The smell of horses fills my nostrils. It inundates my mind with snapshots of dark, wooden buildings, lawns that were always kept green, and flaxen-colored hay bales lining the lane.

"The perpetual pounding of horses' hooves served as the score for summer after summer. Year after year, school came far too soon, and even as the tack rooms emptied, you could still hear the voices of children who had long since grown up but were never really away."

Trick-Riding Begins at Riata

Not everyone at Riata had the ability or the bankroll to compete in horse shows and rodeo or queen contests, so Tom created yet another pursuit: a gymnastics program emphasizing physical fitness. This ancillary program quickly progressed from vaults on a stationary gymnastics horse to trick-riding feats on Riata's real horses. By now Riata Ranch was concentrating just on girls, as Tom realized how few sports opportunities they had. This marked the beginning of the Riata Ranch Cowboy Girls.

The initial trick-riding team was made up of four thirteen-year-old girls. Because they needed a name, Tom dubbed them the Cowboy Girls in honor of their cowboy skills. These girls made such a splash that rodeo producer Cotton Rosser began booking them regularly through his famous rodeo company, The Flying U, and in 1977 he featured Riata in a special rodeo show for Chrysler Corporation's national convention in Reno, Nevada. It was a roaring success, and everyone returned home high on the promise of future engagements.

Another new act was the Riata Ranch Cowboy Girl Band. Music was always important at Riata, and the same high standards were applied to playing the harmonica as competing for a trophy or a title. As a result, Riata's homegrown band was soon performing to rave reviews, from California's famous Cow Palace to New York's Madison Square Garden. Then it went international — enjoying tours across Canada, throughout Europe, and twice to Japan!

Close Calls and Miracles

During this busy time, Tom received notice from his health insurance company that he needed a routine exam. The results proved anything but routine: Stage three melanoma was discovered. Stage four is nearly always terminal. With such a virulent cancer, Tom's only hope for survival was to have surgery immediately.

Shocked and scared, Tom broke the news to a few of his treasured students who were leaving for a horse show, explaining that his and Riata's time might be up. Suddenly Tom's usual invincible outlook deserted him, and he broke down. They all cried together. That was the first and last time Riata saw Tom Maier cry.

Recovery from stage-three melanoma is rare, but Tom's operation proved medically miraculous, for even without chemotherapy, he remains free of cancer to this day. However, Tom has still had to face a number of other formidable medical trials. "It seems every five or ten years Tommy has a bad spell health-wise and wealth-wise," observes Riata's first All-Around Champion, Dr. David Manchester.

In 1983, while helping out at a rodeo in Las Vegas, Nevada, Tom roped a recalcitrant bronc and, in a freak turn of events, his horse was jerked off its feet. Tom came crashing down, hitting his head on a hard surface. It took more than an hour for the ambulance to respond, and the resulting brain damage was traumatic. Upon regaining consciousness, Tom could not walk, talk, or remember things as deeply ingrained as the alphabet.

Left: Kathy Copley shows off her roping style in Japan, 1982.
Above: Renny Spencer performs the Hippodrome, with Jennifer Welch doing the Tail Drag, at the California Rodeo in Salinas.

"When Tom was giving instructions there was no horse I couldn't ride."

— Sharon Gill
Riata girl 1959–1970

Staying on Course

With her captain knocked out of commission, the good ship Riata could have sunk, but instead the crew pulled together and kept her on course. Cotton Rosser kept booking the Cowboy Girls, the girls kept training and wowing audiences, Tom's wife Vickie kept working at her job, his sons helped out at home and away, and everyone kept Tom as active as possible.

"A young girl, Lillis Lancaster, was with me then, and she dedicated her time to my care, along with others," says Tom. "The wonderful thing was the girls never left me home, they'd take me with them everywhere and just sit me down. People who knew me would come by and touch me and talk to me like I was Cheetah, my pet chimpanzee. I remember them touching me, but I couldn't talk, I couldn't answer. . . . It was six months before I was able to communicate with anybody and a full two years before I was solid. A full two years! The thing is, if they'd left me lying alone at home I probably wouldn't have recovered that quickly . . . maybe never. But they didn't, and everything turned out fine.

"Later, in 1994, I had a bout with diverticulitis and was in the hospital for a month. That was very serious, very difficult. . . . At the time, I had a group of ten-year-old girls that I'd got into the movie *Kid's Song*. I remember how special it was coming home to find all of them waiting for me. I'll never forget that.

During the 1980s, the Riata girls honed their performing skills. In the front row, left to right, are Landon Spencer and Renny Spencer; behind them are Niki Evans, Kansas Carradine, and Melissa Solario; and in back is Jennifer Welch.

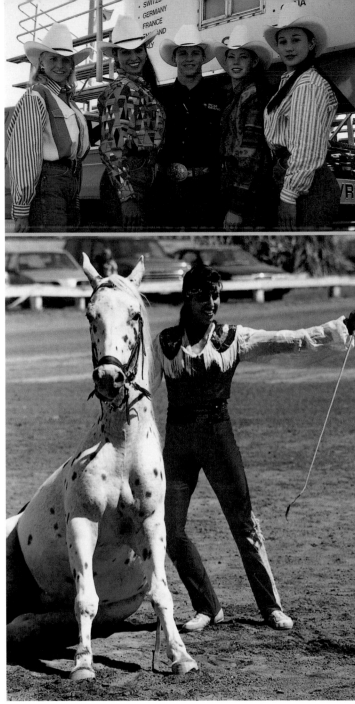

In the 1990s, the Riata girls mingled with the celebrities of the horse world and developed their own specialties. **Top left:** The Riata girls pose with clinician Pat Parelli. **Top right:** The girls appear with seven-time World Champion Cowboy Ty Murray. **Bottom left:** Janna Copley demonstrates Around the World, a rope trick developed at Riata Ranch. **Bottom right:** Lori Alva performs with Rocky, whom she trained to do tricks.

THE ROAD TO RIATA ⇥17⇤

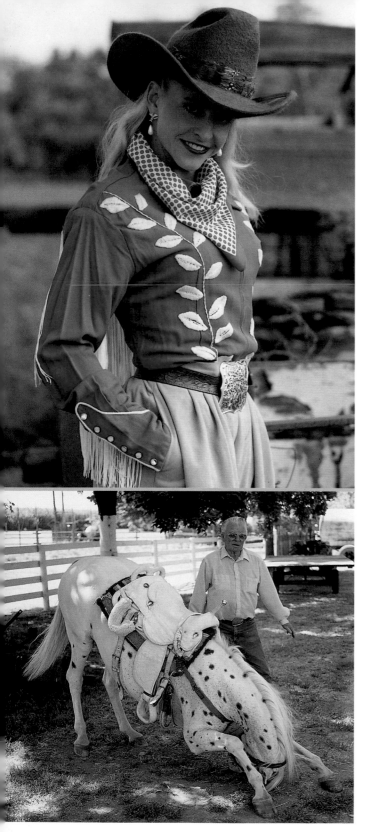

Top: *Jennifer Welch began at Riata Ranch as a horse-crazy ten-year-old; became a superb rider, roper, and performer; and now serves as Tom Maier's partner and business manager.* Bottom: *Tom encourages Rocky to perform a stylish bow.*

> *"I always tell my girls, when you say 'goodbye,' don't look back. Walk away, don't look back."*
>
> — Tom Maier

"Then in 1996, when I came home after my heart surgery, a quadruple bypass, Kansas Carradine and others were waiting to help me up the stairs. So, you see, I'm rarely alone."

As Liz Malloch Doe notes, "Tom's been called a number of times and lived through it." A born survivor with an attitude that life is "fantastic and improving," Tom has proven time and again that he's Riata tough!

Saved by the Code

Tom is tough enough to turn back the Grim Reaper but not tenacious bill collectors. Medical bills from his last two conditions left Tom with enormous debts. A local businessman who admired what Riata did for children arranged a loan of $138,000 in a manner that Tom would be able to repay. The contract for this loan wasn't put down on paper. It was written on the Code of the West: Each gave his word and a handshake to seal the deal.

"A short time later, this gentleman died," Tom reports, sadly. "Wanting to close the estate, his family gave me sixty days to raise the money. A fellow from Texas was helping me and we raised more than $60,000, but I needed more time. The family didn't want to

wait, so they foreclosed. I stayed as long as I could, but then they sold Riata Ranch and I had to leave.

"I'll never forget. *Sixty-four* people from the past came out and helped us move all in one day. Then everybody left and I was the last one to leave the ranch, checking everything out.

"When I drove out of Riata that last time it was like a death. I was alone, and I didn't look back. That was in 1998. I never went back."

TURN AND FACE THE MAGIC

It's apparent from the above accounts that Tom Maier spins Riata magic as deftly as he spins a rope, and those caught in the spell can't help but fall in love with the magician as well. So, when Riata's Merlin calls, his champions rally, spinning their own brand of Riata magic. As Brenda Sampietro recalls, "This past July Tommy called me to ask, 'What are you doing tomorrow?'

"'What do you want me to do?' I replied.

"'Meet me out at the ranch around two o'clock.'

"My breath caught as I asked, 'The ranch you're at now, or the old ranch?'

"'The old ranch.'

"When I drove out to the end of Avenue 300 and crossed those familiar tracks, my heart sank. It was a mess . . . nothing had been done for two years. Tommy greeted me with, 'We've got to get it cleaned up.'

"'No problem, I'll start calling. . .'

Brenda explains, "The new owner had evidently fielded so many inquiries about Riata

Ranch that he came to realize that he'd bought much more than a ranch; he'd purchased *hallowed ground.*" Graciously, generously, he invited Riata back home.

"That weekend we had two groups out: one Saturday, one Sunday," Brenda continues. "We hacked weeds, hauled trash, pruned trees, and got stung by bees. . . . It was great!"

"Then we heard the train whistle, and we remembered how Tommy had taught us to turn our horses toward the train so they wouldn't spook. By the time the engine arrived we were all there, up on the arena rail with our rakes and hoes, facing the train like we did when we were ten years old . . . back where we belong . . . at Riata."

Jennifer Welch welcomes Cynthia Beltran, later nicknamed Tiger, and her mother to Riata Ranch on Cynthia's first day.

Tiger's Diary

October 11

When we first went out to Riata Ranch we thought it was just some ordinary riding school. They don't only teach riding, but they also teach calisthenics and social graces. On my first day I started riding with someone behind me to help me, and soon I was riding all by myself. I loved it, and I will be back!

Tiger

From the Ground Up

For youngsters with cowboy dreams, horses — particularly Riata's fast, flashy mounts — are powerful magnets. Having scores of excited, inexperienced young people around such big, quick animals is risky business, however, so Riata instills safety, discipline, and order from day one by ritualizing work and training routines.

At Riata, horsemanship doesn't begin with the horse. It's learned from the ground up, starting with chores that are fine-tuned until they are almost like religious rites. All tasks, even those that seem inconsequential, are perfected into precise protocols. Through education, trial, and error, techniques evolve until the safest, most effective process develops. Tom Maier often makes the distinction, "It's not *my* way, it's *the* way." The Riata Way.

The "Riata Rake," for example, creates an effect that is a combination of a Zen sand garden and the groomed checkerboard surface of a Major League baseball field. This efficient raking routine originated in 1963, when David Manchester and Richard Harris were first working at Bass Lake. On weekends

Kansas Carradine and Cynthia "Tiger" Beltran make friends with an Appaloosa foal. Appaloosas and Paints are the horses of choice for Riata performances because of their distinctive looks and tolerant dispositions.

Tom held inspection and was never totally pleased with the state of the grounds. In an effort to impress Tom once and for all, Richard created what is now known as "the Pattern": raking the entire yard in even stripes first one way, then the other, to create an orderly herringbone pattern. Finally, the grounds displayed a striking military precision that made it obvious that the students were taking proper pains with their work, earning Tom's characteristically understated yet cherished praise, "Hey . . . the place looks all right."

Neophytes often miss the point of the herringbone pattern, for it seems laughably compulsive to insist on a prescribed design for a chore that seems as mundanely insignificant as raking. Yet for that very reason, the Riata Rake has become a lighthearted symbol of Riata's high standards, underscoring the point that there are no insignificant jobs. If something needs to be done, it's to be done well.

Taking Pride in Perfection

Jennifer Welch, Tom's valued assistant, a noted trick-rider, and a Riata regular of twenty-six years, says with a smile, "The object is to clean the ground of leaves, but it's more than that. When we all have a rake in our hands, we're all on the same level. Everyone who ever came to Riata had to rake a stall or the lane, so it's a common denominator of being here . . . an outgrowth of the feeling of Riata. It's *pride.* Alums brag that they still do the Riata Rake in their own gardens and yards."

When Riata students are working, there is an unusual, almost cathedral-like quiet — no genial banter, no giggling, no small talk. They

Above: *A rake and a shovel are part of every girl's life at Riata Ranch.* ***Opposite:*** *As other girls rake the lane, Cynthia Beltran walks her horse to cool him off.*

> *"I take the values I learned here with me every day of my life."*
>
> — Teresa Ogas
> **Riata girl 1987–1992**

do their jobs wordlessly because they're concentrating on doing their best. There is no such thing as mindless work at Riata: All work has import and purpose. And since so much is done around livestock, where distractions can be dangerous, you must remain mindful of what's going on around you or you could get hurt. The work is serious because, in the end, the risk is serious. Thus, like a troupe of telepathic novitiates, Cowboy Girls perform their systematic chores as a totally absorbed, silently efficient, perfectly choreographed team.

CARING FOR THE HORSES

Since Riata's programs revolve around horses, proper care of the animals is paramount. Like horsemanship, horse care doesn't start with the horse. It goes from the ground up, starting with the stall. To keep an animal, you must maintain a healthy environment for it. At Riata, cleaning the stall is not just a chore; like raking, it's a matter of pride.

"We're very particular about how we clean stalls," Jennifer explains. "Our stalls are sand-based, and we're careful not to throw out any clean, serviceable bedding with the waste. At home or away, people comment how clean

The Cowboy Girls rarely chat to one another while they do their daily chores. Here Kelly Mancha is focused, absorbed, and efficient.

and neat our stalls and stable area always are. This is one of the first jobs that builds pride."

Hoof Care

The cryptic cowboy slogan "No hoof, no horse" sums up the vital chore of caring for hooves. Riata's trick horses are not ridden for long distances on hard terrain, so they can be kept barefoot with a simple regimen of cleaning, trimming, oiling, and treating hooves as needed. For long parade venues on asphalt, borium shoes are put on to protect the hooves and keep horses from slipping. Otherwise, the farrier simply trims the hooves, carefully rasping the toe to a slightly rounded edge to prevent chipping.

GROOMING SECRETS

The key to show grooming is to take care of your horse as if you're going to a show every day. This way, you get into the habit of good grooming, and if, for example, the mane needs trimming or training, it will be ready by showtime.

Clipping

California's temperatures rarely descend below freezing, but Riata's performances often take the troupe to the Midwest or back East while the weather is still very cold. To allow for mild training weather and still guard against colder climates, Riata's mounts are given a special body-clip, which trims hair on the legs, face, neck, and most of the torso

Cynthia Beltran cleans her horse's hooves with a hoof pick. Riata horses go barefoot most of the time, wearing shoes only for long parades on hard pavement.

except under the saddle and over the rump. Trimming shaggy winter hair gives a neater, well-groomed look, and the horses can be blanketed for warmth as needed.

Braiding

The Cowboy Girls braid their horses' manes and/or tails for a number of reasons. Braiding protects the hair's fullness and length; it keeps the tail clean and maintained for shows; it reduces tangling, soiling, and breakage; it helps train unruly manes; and it saves time since the protected braids may be left in for a few days at a time.

Bathing

Riata horses are not bathed after every training session. The decision to bathe them depends on the level of work done, time considerations (time is usually tight for the girls during school weeks), and the weather. A hard workout on a warm day usually ends with a bath, and during the hot summer months a favorite activity following an active lesson is to take the horses down to the river for bathing or tail dragging.

Regardless of the temperature, a Riata horse is always cooled out, groomed, and put up clean and dry. The girls do pre- and post-ride checks of the horses, paying particular attention to physical condition, especially that of the legs, and overall cleanliness.

Opposite: Bathing is a treat for horses and people on a dusty summer day in the San Joaquin Valley. **Top right:** *Lacey Coelho shows Cynthia Beltran how to braid her horse's tail for an upcoming performance.* **Bottom right:** *Amanda Welty combs her horse's mane a few strands at a time, being careful not to pull out too many hairs.*

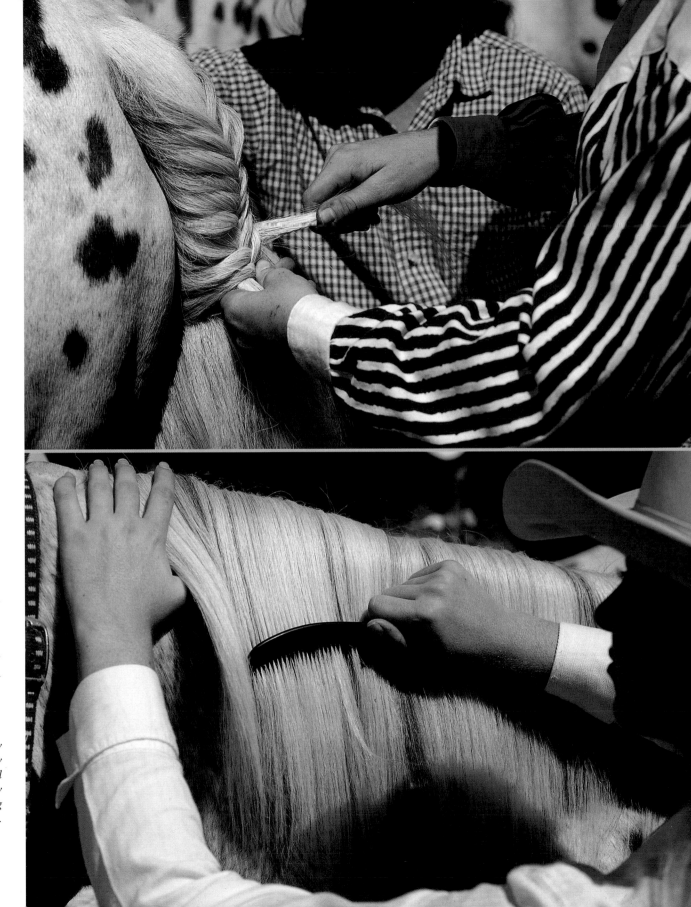

"When I was first at Riata, if you were caught putting your horse up with sweat behind its ears your name was put up on the bulletin board," recalls Jennifer. "You'd never do that again! But here, it's a matter of pride to put your horse away clean and nice with no sweat marks."

Riata's flashy white Leopard Appaloosas demand a bit more diligent cleaning, since stains are obvious against their light coats. Jennifer laughs as she reveals Riata's horse-whitening secret: "Mrs. Stewart's Bluing. It's an old-time whitener still available in most supermarkets' laundry departments. You mix it in with your shampoo, sponge it on, and rinse immediately . . . if you leave it on too long your horse will turn blue. But for horses that are badly stained, we put the bluing on directly and leave it until the stain fades away."

FEEDING FOR HEALTH AND PERFORMANCE

The feeding regimen at Riata is vital to the entire program, for without healthy horses everything would come to a screeching stop quicker than a reining champion. Since Riata horses have to be performance-fit, ready to

Regular routines are at the core of the Riata program. **Top left, middle left, and bottom left:** *Girls administer seasonal vaccinations and brush and prepare their horses for Saturday classes.* **Above:** *Cynthia Beltran feeds Rocky.* **Opposite:** *Jennifer Welch, Laurie McWilliams, and Kansas Carradine feed their horses behind the scenes at Equitana USA.*

haul over long distances on short notice, and quick to acclimate to new and often chaotic situations, a reliable, sound feeding program is critical. Tom likes a good basic routine adjusted to meet each animal's individual needs. Being blessed with good San Joaquin Valley oat hay, the ranch has made that the basic feed for all. Since the horses are never worked hard or long, oat hay provides the proper nutrition without the extra protein and energy boosts that alfalfa and grain supply.

However, like people, no two horses have the same appetite or nutritional needs, so the eating habits of the remuda, or herd, are closely monitored. If one horse doesn't finish its feed, or another is looking around for more after eating, programs are adjusted accordingly. Occasionally a few of the horses need a little something extra and are given supplemental grain, vitamins, or other nutrients.

On-the-Road Care

Horses must be in good physical and mental form to withstand the disruption and stress of long hauls, so when Riata mounts are on the road, every horse gets grain with a precautionary dose of electrolytes. Commonly used to guard against dehydration, electrolytes are administered at Riata to ward off effects caused by the fact that horses do not urinate while moving. Maintaining equilibrium during hauling requires continuous rebalancing. The horses are thus in a constant state of tension, which prevents the relaxation required for urinating.

Left: Halters always hang with the lead rope on the left for efficient use. Opposite: The Riata tack room is the center of life at the ranch and is always kept orderly and immaculate.

This, coupled with the fact that standing in the same position for long periods may lead to fatigue or soreness, makes it crucial to stop every four to six hours for a five- to ten-minute break. The girls take the horses out to walk, stretch, or void; shovel out the trailer; replenish feed, water, grain, and supplements as needed; and then load the horses back up and move on.

SHINING SADDLES

Some of the best saddles ever made hang proudly in Riata's tack room and, as a result of careful maintenance and repair over the decades, the Cowboy Girls can still hang proudly — and securely — from their aged straps. With more than twenty-two saddles, Riata Ranch has one of the largest collections of trick-riding saddles in the world, including two full sets of authentic N. Porter and Monroe Veach saddles.

Depending on the visual effect desired, the girls choose the natural brown or the snappy white saddles for their performances. Since the saddles date back to the 1930s or 1940s, even the tack at Riata Ranch offers lessons in time-honored preservation versus throw-away consumption. Restoring the real thing sure beats replacing it with anything less.

Because the white saddles are used most often, routine tack care becomes time-intensive. In addition to providing the careful deep cleaning and conditioning that a brown leather saddle requires, the Cowboy Girls

Opposite: The trick-rider's lifeline is her tack. From left, Cynthia Beltran, Jennifer Welch, Paula Herrera, Kelly Mancha, and Idalia Reveles care for their saddles.

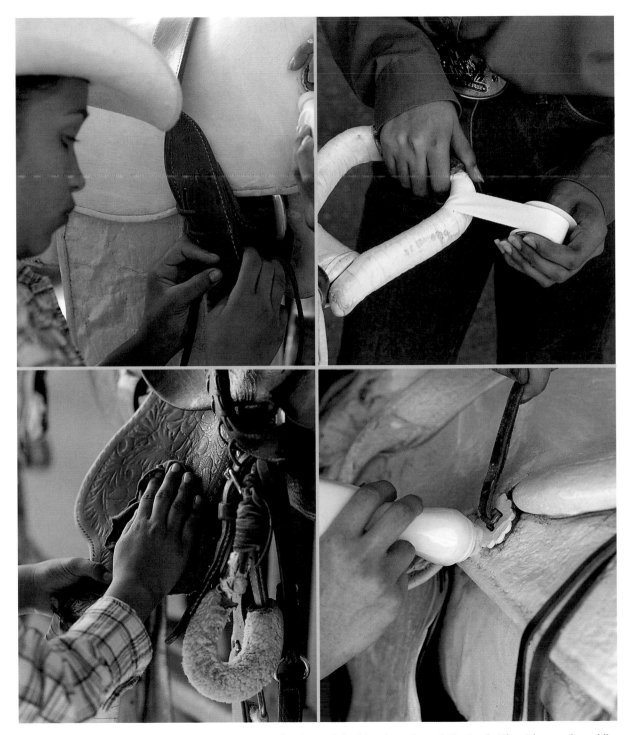

Cleaning and checking the tack are daily rituals. The girls treat the saddles with respect, whether (clockwise from top left) they are checking the laces, taping a stirrup, applying white polish, or oiling a fender.

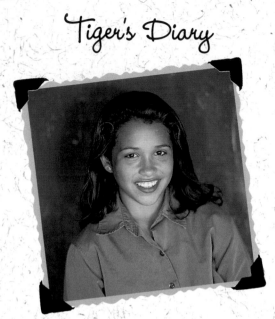

Tiger's Diary

November 3

Riata Ranch takes girls all over the world trick-riding and trick-roping. They get to be on TV shows, magazines, and the best part of all is that they get to meet important people and experience the world. I thought to myself, "That's what I want to do." I'm staying with Riata Ranch for that.

Tiger

must coat the white saddles with almost a full bottle of white shoe polish, let them dry, then buff them with a cloth.

"During regular training periods at home, a careful wipe-down and touch-up suffice," says Jennifer. "But white is unforgiving, so when we're performing or practicing a lot, our saddles are cleaned every time. We also have to re-tape the horn and the handles in such a way as to achieve a good grip, with no unraveling or loose ends. It all takes time and practice. To properly wash, condition, polish, and tape a saddle takes about two hours."

SAFETY FIRST

In all Riata training the basic tenet is, as former Cowboy Girl Kathy Copley recites, "Safety first averts disaster." This is where ritualized habits really pay off. For instance, the San Joaquin Valley Railroad runs right alongside Riata's riding arena. Horses spooked by the train or its whistle could wreak havoc during classes. To avert that possibility, Riata students are taught always to turn their horses to face the train. Like the Riata Rake, this has become a signature routine ingraining the safety habit in Riata riders. Automatically turning an agitated horse to face a spooky object diffuses a lot of potentially dangerous incidents.

"It still amazes me that when our horses are running free in the pasture, they'll race away or kick up their heels at the passing train," observes Jennifer. "But when we're riding those same horses and we stop to face that train, not one of them even flinches!"

Safety awareness saturates life at the

> ### "We need more places like this in the world."
> — Joanna Herrera-Howard
> Riata girl 1978–1994

ranch, says Laurie McWilliams, one of Riata's original trick-riders. "Safety at Riata is a way of being that's built into everything we do," she says. "It's part of branding the cattle, it's part of starting the colts . . . it's just part of the whole background of ranch life. It's not necessarily a set of rules that we follow; it's 'Pay attention! Look at that horse — he's ready to bite, or kick, or run, or whatever.' From the very start you learn to watch an animal's body language until it becomes instinctive. So Riata's safety program is, 'Be aware!' It obviously works because hundreds have gone through Riata and injuries are incredibly minimal."

Training Horses to Focus

To be safe, a trick-riding horse must be honest. If the horse is distracted from his job by the crowd, arena events, or an open gate, it can spell disaster for the rider who depends on him to run straight and true. To that end, training protocols are designed to desensitize and discipline the horse, while supporting his honesty and natural calm.

Facing the train is one of the methods for desensitizing the horse to alarming distractions. Another steadfast safety discipline is to circle at the gate before exiting the arena. "A Riata horse is never — and I mean *never* — allowed to leave the training arena until he

Opposite: Before leaving the round corral, Cynthia "Tiger" Beltran always circles her horse. This is part of the training system at Riata Ranch.

first circles at the gate," Jennifer reiterates. "That routine is put into a horse's mind from the first day he's with us to prevent incidents where a horse runs out or stops at a gate during a performance. That simple technique establishes in our horses' minds the certainty that they may not leave the arena until cued by circling. As a result our horses are not distracted by gates."

When asked about his training techniques Tom says, "Horses understand our methods." By this he means that Riata understands horses, after decades of working in partnership with them.

THE IMPORTANCE OF RITUALS

Having to work the Riata Way may sound dogmatic. It is, and in that lie its strength and success. Distilled through years of experience, the Riata procedures consistently produce excellent results, safely and efficiently. Thus, a master/teacher/elder can relinquish responsibility to a student, secure in the knowledge that the method supports the student in executing the task properly.

Once learned, each sanctioned routine is then easily and exactly passed from student to student, producing and reproducing the same excellence. You can bank on it. Since the safety, security, and success of Riata's students and livestock all depend on these tried-and-true techniques, banking on excellence is the only way to go — the Riata Way.

Left: After every training session the girls walk the horses to cool them off. **Opposite:** *The horses are turned out to relax at the end of a long day.*

Learning the Ropes

"The tracks at the entrance to Riata may look like ordinary railroad tracks," notes Jennifer Welch. "But crossing those rails has become a symbol that brings a surge of excited anticipation that you're on track to becoming a Riata Ranch Cowboy Girl. You know that once you cross that steel you'll be put to the test. You just don't know *how,* yet."

Personal tests are the essence of Riata Ranch and, like horses, they entice young people. Nowadays many parents try to protect their children from unexpected, risky, or tough tests by paving the way for their young ones on the road of life. By doing so, they risk overprotecting their children and underestimating their abilities. Tom Maier doesn't make that mistake.

Tom attracts young people like a Pied Piper not because he coddles them but because he challenges them. Their minds, bodies, and spirits are constantly tested by new tasks, responsibilities, risks, and adventures. Riata's imaginatively innovative programs provide the stimulation, security, and success that allow children to grow, mature, and blossom. Like new shoots seeking the sun, Riata students grow straight and strong, fed on challenge, grounded in competence, and sustained by the warm glow of success.

Jennifer Welch gives a roping lesson to a group of Riata students. Tom Maier
introduced roping to students to give them something difficult to do and
thus teach them the concept of tenacity.

Blazing Your Own Trail

Tom recognizes that life's true adventure lies in carving out your own trail even when the terrain is difficult or dangerous. He knows that in the very act of blazing that tough track, one develops strength of character and discovers the meaning of life. The reward emerges when a youngster looks back down that rugged, hand-hewn trail and realizes how far she's come . . . *by herself.* As Janna Copley recalls, "The hardest part of Riata was training and working long hours in the Valley heat or in mud or in winter, when my toes were numb from the frost and I'd have to keep going, pushing myself to the limits." She pauses. "That was also the *best* part."

Parents can't *give* accomplishment and personal pride to a child. No one can. To earn that, the child must do for herself. Each must risk her own destiny. As Tom observes, "The person who risks nothing, gains nothing and becomes nothing. Only a person who risks is truly free."

SETTING A GOAL, ACHIEVING A DREAM

The girls' day starts in Riata's courtyard with the morning meeting, where duties, activities, and performances are discussed. Quick and efficient, these daily touchstone gatherings last only five to twenty minutes yet are vital to creating the day's harmony in work and scheduling. Meetings also provide an opportunity to review individual and common goals, which support directed team-building.

Dream Incubator

Goals are one of Riata's most important tools. Youngsters often hear family or teachers say, "Dare to dream. You can be anything you want." At Riata, youngsters learn how to make that happen. Riata Ranch is a dream incubator, helping each student achieve dreams by setting goals.

"With me, everybody must have a goal," declares Tom. "Everybody. Without a goal you have no idea where you're going. Like the magnetic-north heading on a compass, a goal gives you direction. For example, Devon Collins was a girl who came to Riata when she was eleven. One day I saw her outside after class, crying. Thinking she might be hurt, I asked what was wrong.

"She said, 'Everyone has a goal except me.'

"'Oh, come on,' I said. 'You're so tall and pretty you could be a model!' Now I'd just

Left: Awareness is the key to success at Riata Ranch. From left, Kelly Mancha, Paula Herrera, Cynthia Beltran, Idalia Reveles, Lacey Coelho, Jennifer Welch, and Tasha Candela watch a roping demonstration. Opposite: A typical scene at Riata Ranch in the morning. Morning meetings are held so that everyone knows the day's activities and goals.

"I joined Riata Ranch when I was eleven years old, and it changed my life."

— Teresa Ogas
Riata girl 1987–1992

pulled that out of the air to comfort her, but that little girl took that goal and ran with it. She became California's Appaloosa Queen and then went on to the Nationals! Eileen Ford, from the Ford Modeling Agency, saw pictures of her competing and sent out a contract. Devon signed on, moved to New York, and worked as a successful model for a long time. That shows the power of a goal. Oh, yes, *everybody's* got to have a goal!"

Tom often asks, "What do you see yourself doing in ten years?" This encourages forward thinking. Look ahead, determine your dream, then start laying down the tracks to get to it by way of acquiring necessary skills.

Step by Step to Success

Once their goals are defined, Riata girls learn to plot their "personal compass course" to that chosen ambition. They do this by determining what skills they need to develop, then breaking down the ultimate goal into progressively attainable milestones. What's your goal for the next six months? What can you do in school to further this goal? What physical attributes do you need to achieve it?

Work on this, improve that, do this, do that. It's not easy, but it's effective!

So effective that Riata lost a valuable Cowboy Girl to this process after twenty-three years of service at the Ranch. Kathy Copley came to Riata in 1969 at the age of eight and worked her way up through the ranks, earning leadership positions in the band and on the trick-riding and trick-roping teams.

"One of the basic philosophies of the ranch is always to do your best, then strive to improve; follow your strengths and work on your weaknesses," says Kathy. "That's why I left Riata. When I looked forward ten years as Tom always told us to do, I saw I wouldn't really be improving myself any more. So I went back to school, got a Ph.D. in biochemistry, and now I'm on my second career, as a biochemist with a pharmaceutical company."

Riata's alums are honest with themselves, motivated to succeed, and confident enough to spread their wings and fly.

Learning from Each Other

Another effective teaching tool that was born out of necessity at Riata is peer education and support. With sixty to ninety students at the ranch and no other adult trainers, Tom had advanced students teach those coming up through the ranks. This proved inspired for a number of reasons. Like its wise parent, mentorship, and its mighty cousin, peer pressure, youth-to-youth training is powerful stuff. Kids want to belong, so they'll eagerly follow the lead of accomplished friends to gain, and bask in, the support of a coveted peer group.

Tom Maier instructs a beginner class. Every Riata student must have a goal, both in riding and in life.

Peer training not only teaches the subject at hand, but it also fosters respect for achievement and seniority, gives older students leadership experience, and establishes that advancement is earned only by merit. As Tom explains, "I never *give* anybody anything. They have to earn it. At Riata, class levels and promotion are not based on age, they're based on ability. Otherwise, new girls wouldn't have the respect of the team. A team's built on mutual respect, and that respect must be earned."

Taking Pride in Yourself

Riata's peer training combined with natural peer pressure led to peer discipline, reinforcing personal actions. As a result, very few disciplinary issues come up, because students respect the program, each other, and Tom. External punishment is rarely needed, since the threat of internal punishment, the feeling of disappointing herself, her team members, or Tom, usually keeps a student on track.

"This system instills so much natural discipline and respect that whatever task you are assigned to, it is accepted that you do it," Jennifer reports. "You want to do the right thing. Even something as basic as morning roll call; nobody ever wants to be late because if you are, everyone knows. These are great lessons at a really young age that stay with you: showing up on time, being responsible for your own work. Even today, I hate to be late."

Christina Dalton-Newsome, Cowboy Girl from 1963 to 1975, agrees. "Tom provided many things at the ranch. The biggest were discipline and punctuality. I remember

him lecturing to be on time or five minutes early each riding day. You learned responsibility because you were in charge of an animal that depended on you. You learned to take pride in what you did and in yourself. You were in competition with the others to be the best, but at the same time you took care of each other. You learned to accept defeat and go on to the next hurdle."

Earning a Place on the Team

Thus, Riata's training program builds knowledge, ability, discipline, and respect as students progress through successive levels of education and accomplishment. The initial program, Horses, Girls & More, lays a solid foundation in physical fitness, Western and trick equitation, horsemanship, and introductory roping. Each prospective Cowboy Girl must learn, perform, and prove herself through each training level, thereby gaining the respect and trust of the entire Riata team.

Girls who demonstrate that they have the talent and commitment to advance to team membership are rewarded with more intensive instruction in roping, horsemastership, and ranch and road management. New team members invest many hours at the ranch and on the road as the support crew for the performing Cowboy Girls, who in turn help them polish their roping and trick-riding skills. Once a team member acquires consistent talent and stage presence, she's worked into the performance line-up, finally winning her own place as a Riata Ranch Cowboy Girl.

★ Life Lessons ★

Brenda Sampietro
(Cowboy Girl from 1958 to 1964)

"When we learned, we learned to do everything," says Brenda Sampietro. "Not just how to tack up and the names for all the parts of the saddle, bridle, and harnesses, but how to tan leather so we'd really understand types and qualities of hides and how best to care for it. There was no end to the learning experience at Riata."

Deep Learning

The training process reflects Tom's comprehensive approach to education. Subjects are explored to such depth that students not only learn, but they also *understand.*

"Our whole concept is built around total awareness," says Jennifer. "We learn from the best trick-riders, to be sure, but we also learn from talented vaulters, dressage trainers, reining champions, and even Russian Cossacks! We explore everything remotely related to what we do, decide what works, then incorporate it into our training. I don't know of any other equestrian organization that combines so many elements from so many different disciplines as we do."

Although his formal education ended with seventh grade, Tom has always had a hunger for learning. Through mentoring, listening, and open awareness, he's fostered a comprehensive educational experience where students learn a subject beyond knowing it; they learn to the point of comprehending it. As a result, at Riata they don't just train, they explain; they don't just instruct, they demonstrate; they don't just teach, they mentor; they don't just educate, they enlighten; they don't just imagine, they perform; they don't just encourage, they inspire; they don't just set goals, they take aim and hit their targets.

*Top left: Every Riata girl learns to handle a rope cowboy-style to enhance her trick-roping skills. **Bottom left:** Tom Maier shares tips with (from left) Paula Herrera, Jennifer Welch, Sarah Ewing, Lacey Coelho, and Idalia Reveles. **Opposite:** Idalia, Kelly Mancha, Paula, Jennifer, and Cynthia Beltran work on the art of trick-roping.*

Dancing Ropes

Once you hit that first bull's eye, you set your sights on the next. At Riata there's no room for complacency. The bar is always being raised, horizons are always being expanded, and abilities are always being stretched, until there's nothing that's too high, too distant, or too hard to achieve. As Janna Copley learned, "If you say 'I can't,' you'll never learn what you *can* do."

Janna speaks from experience, since the acid test for persistence is found in the vexing art of trick-roping. In fact, Tom says he introduced roping precisely for the challenge it presented. He felt things were coming too easily, and he wanted the girls to develop tenacity.

Sixteen-year-old Paula Herrera, a current Cowboy Girl, reports on her roping initiation. "When I was learning to trick-rope it seemed impossible for me to jump into the loop. When it was my turn during practice drill I'd hesitate, hopping on one leg, but not making the jump into the rope, and then I'd give up and pass. Tom started calling me a one-legged flamingo, and that's what made me change. I finally realized if other girls do it then it's possible, and I could do it, too." That small jump became a big leap for Paula from impossible to possible, then on to performing success.

Using Both Mind *and* Body

While talented Cowboy Girls make dancing with a spinning rope look enticingly easy, it's actually an extremely exacting skill demanding focused attention, fluid motion, precise rhythm, and years of practice. Progression through the Red, White, Blue, Silver, and Gold levels of Riata's roping ranks can be dishearteningly slow. It usually takes more than a year of concentrated effort before a girl ropes well enough to start performing.

"Each level has its own skills, from Red's most basic on through to the most advanced in Silver," says Jennifer. "The highest level, Gold, is based more on achievement than on skills. It recognizes what you give back to trick-roping and the interest you put into it as an individual. No one's earned Gold, yet.

"What most people don't understand about learning to rope is that it's much more

mental than physical," she explains. "You're telling your body how to stand, what to do with your arms, when to jump in, how fast to spin for Rollovers, Ocean Waves, or the Texas Skip. You have to think about everything *consciously* until it's planted firmly enough to become *subconscious*. Plus, depending on the weather or different climates, the rope feels and acts differently from one day to the next. It can get pretty frustrating."

Beginner's Luck

Janna Copley recalls a session with the late Western star, Montie Montana, that brought home this point for her. "I asked Montie to teach me the Texas Skip. He got a rope appropriate for my height and showed me what to do. I spun it and followed his instructions so carefully that I did four jumps through it on the first try! Since the Texas Skip is touted as one of the hardest trick-roping stunts, I was thrilled with the results . . . and the fact that *Montie Montana* taught me was icing on the cake!

"Montie said, 'Well now, that was great! You should have that trick down in about a year.' Confused, I thought, A year? I just did it four times! It took me a while to understand that he meant I had a long way to go before I'd have the *consistent skill* to perform at a show in full costume with crowds, wind, lights, distractions. Beginner's luck isn't mastery. That lesson has served me in a lot of areas of my life: sports, jobs, relationships. They all take time and repetition to master."

Left: Paula Herrera and Cynthia Beltran practice a timing skill called Handstand and Catch. Opposite: Riata alumnae Janna Copley and Laurie McWilliams demonstrate the finer points of the Texas Skip to the current Cowboy Girls.

Creating a Spectacle

Since Riata specializes in thrilling crowds, difficult and seemingly impossible acts are a hallmark of the Rafter-Double-R brand. Having invented choreographed team-trick-roping, the team is constantly setting, and re-setting, the standard in this line of entertainment.

"When we first started, we just roped with everyone doing her own tricks, since that was the way it had always been done by the greats like Will Rogers, Vince Bruce, and Montie Montana," explains Jennifer. "But then we wondered if we could take something that's been around so long, repackage it, and make it seem brand new.

"First of all, there'd never been a girls' trick-roping team before, so that was new and different. Then we created staged roping routines using rock-and-roll, jazz, or Western music, depending on our theme. Finally, we choreographed the whole thing until now our routines are really pretty technical. Having to trick-rope to the beat of the music while dancing as a team is much harder than just roping. We took that old Western art form and turned it into theater."

When former ropers Janna Copley and Laurie McWilliams returned to Riata after being away a few years and saw what was up, they exclaimed, "Oh my gosh, now you have to dance to it, too?" They were impressed by how complex an already difficult act had become. But then, that's the Riata Way — keep raising that bar!

*Top: This routine, Around the World, was developed at Riata Ranch in honor of the team's international travels. **Bottom:** The Riata trick-roping routines are choreographed to music. Here Jennifer Welch, Laurie McWilliams, Kansas Carradine, and Janna Copley perform synchronized Texas Skips.*

The girls make their own ropes using methods passed on by their mentor Montie Montana. They first put a hondo (an "eye" or loop) onto a cotton rope. The rope is then hung and stretched to remove kinks. **Top left:** *Jennifer Welch stretches a hondo into a rope, on a device passed on by Montie Montana.* **Bottom left and above:** *The girls rub the rope with pieces of burlap to smooth it out. By using these methods, they develop a feel for when a rope is right for trick-roping.*

"I was fearless because I know that Tom understood better than I just how far I could go."

— Sharon Gill
Riata girl 1959–1970

Tom firmly believes, "If you can dream it, you can do it. I know, because we do things that most people never even try. When you accomplish a difficult task that you don't think you can do, it's like being a tiny frog that jumps so high and true that it can land on the top of a pole. For years now Riata's been helping people do the impossible . . . wild things from breaking a zebra to ride to trick-riding around the world." He smiles. "At Riata, we keep putting frogs on poles."

GIRL POWER

Daring Cowboy Girls know all about jumping high and landing precisely . . . on and off charging horses! Physical training is the foundation of trick-riding, and supple strength must be built up slowly for each girl to progress and excel safely. Like adding weights to a backpack, strength and training routines are developed gradually, always building on what's gone before until a student is physically, mentally, and emotionally able to balance the full load.

Because of anatomical differences, girls have to work harder than boys do to gain the upper body strength necessary for proper lift in vaulting on and off a horse. Riata has efficiently integrated this aspect of training into the daily routine. Students gain strength through work rather than through isolated calisthenics.

As Jennifer points out, "We do so much physical activity at the Ranch that there's no

Opposite: Cynthia Beltran practices her roping technique in a shady barn with only her horse as audience.

need for a separate exercise program. Raking the lane, cleaning stalls, lifting loaded pitch forks, shoveling manure, sweeping patios, moving hay bales . . . these all build the upper body strength needed for roping and the various balance and ground tricks in trick-riding."

Tom and Jennifer use the mini-trampoline and the vaulting barrel, or stationary gymnastic horse, to teach the tricks and develop position, posture, and control in the legs, arms, and head. This equipment simulates "lift" so the girls learn to control it before they're dealing with a horse.

"The first time someone experiences lift they usually get scared, go blank, close their eyes, and hope they land okay," states Jennifer. "That's when you can get hurt. At Riata, the girls practice the motions of each trick dozens and dozens and *dozens* of times before progressing to a live horse. Then they repeat the same maneuvers hundreds more times at successive gaits until they achieve proficiency at the walk, the trot, the lope, and finally the performance gallop."

The Sweet Smile of Success

As the girls train, Tom and Jennifer watch closely. It is rare for either to offer praise. Tom is hard on the girls, often barking "Do it again!" if he is unsatisfied with a first attempt. The girl will try again. When she finally gets it right, Tom says nothing, but the girl senses her accomplishment from the inside, and a small, private smile appears on her face.

Such consistent repetition implants the proper actions and responses in the rider's mind; for in trick-riding, safety resides in practiced rhythm and split-second timing.

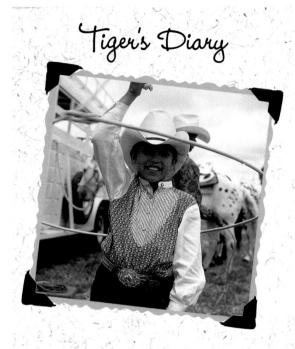

Tiger's Diary

December 10

Today they started me on the roping. I really wasn't good at that. The roping is the hardest thing we do, and it's so frustrating. I am really fast at everything I do and I think in order to get better I am going to have to learn to slow down!

Tiger

"Riata, simply put, means 'Do something with your life.' There is nothing you cannot do."

— Lisa Wylie
Riata girl 1969–1979

*Below: Running alongside the horse not only improves rhythm and timing but also deepens the bond between human and animal. Here Cynthia Beltran trains with her horse, Tomahawk. **Opposite:** Kansas Carradine performs the Backbend. In order to pass to the next level of training, a Cowboy Girl must perform each trick perfectly, five times in a row. Riata adopted this policy since doing a trick at home with no pressure is very different from performing in an arena before thousands of spectators. With consistent mastery, if a girl gets nervous and her emotions take over, she will have enough automatically programmed skill to get by.*

Bonding with the Horse

To gain that rhythm and timing on a moving horse, each girl logs miles in the round corral, trotting or running beside her mount until the animal's gait becomes her own. The goal is to train the horse to "rate" itself — maintaining a consistent pace and a calm demeanor at every speed — and then to stop smoothly and correctly. Once rider and horse are in sync, the vaults and trick-riding can begin. A vigorous aerobic workout for a rider, running beside a free horse is also an emotional charge and a profound bonding experience between species. This is where the all-important psychic connection between horse and rider is solidified.

Training in the Round Corral

Trick-riders don't train by doing tricks over and over in a large arena as they do in a performance; most training takes place in a 70-foot-diameter round corral. The only time the arena is used is to train a horse to run the pattern or to give a new rider the feeling of a full arena run. Otherwise, everyday basic training takes place in the round corral, where horses and riders can circle freely without the restriction of a longe line.

TACKING UP FOR TRICK-RIDING

Methodical care and proper maintenance are particularly important where tack is concerned, because tack is a trick-rider's lifeline. A Cowboy Girl performing on a charging horse has no safety net beyond her gear. Thus, like a sky-diver packing his or her own parachute, each girl is responsible for maintaining and checking her own gear, which Tom then double-checks.

Learning the Hard Way

This lesson was highlighted for former Cowboy Girl Kathy Copley during a show in Atlanta, Georgia, in 1981. She was to perform a Tail Drag — stretched out, hanging backward over the rump of her galloping horse. As soon as she flung herself back, she realized to her horror that the foot straps were set long, so her head and shoulders fell too low — into the path of her horse's hammering hooves.

In an instant Kathy was knocked unconscious, and as the horse charged back to its station, her limp body was kicked again and again. She came to in the hospital, badly bruised but in one piece and very grateful that Riata's horses don't wear steel shoes!

Stiff and sore, she nonetheless felt well enough to perform the next day but had trouble getting her left arm to work properly. "What an odd sensation when you expect your arm to move naturally and it doesn't

Cynthia Beltran prepares to trick-ride. Every Riata girl, even the smallest, totes her own saddle.

happen," Kathy laughs. "I couldn't figure out what was wrong." Back home, her doctor discovered that she had detached a few shoulder ligaments.

"Everything healed fine, but I know that accident should never have happened," she admits. "Tom wasn't with us at that show, and I hadn't followed the safety procedure of pre-checking my straps and position for the Tail Drag with my horse standing still. I *assumed* the straps were properly set. Obviously, they weren't. It was my responsibility to be sure, and I messed up."

Jennifer Welch sets out the saddle blankets to be used for the day's activities.

Each Riata girl must pass a saddling test. Here the girls place the pad (top left), hoist up the saddle (top right), adjust it (bottom left), and tighten the cinch (bottom right).

TRAINING THE TRICK-RIDING HORSE

The Cowboy Girls are famous for thrilling performances on well-trained horses. Recently at Sacramento's California State Fair, Troy Ellerman, one of the world's top trick-riders, made a point of complimenting the discipline of Riata's horses and how well they ran the pattern.

Yet again, Riata's success is the result of a carefully developed system. In trick-riding the horse runs a simple oval pattern, similar to a miniature racetrack. Instead of standing at a starting gate, each horse stands with the rest of Riata's team at one end of the arena, called "the station," until Tom cues its rider and they blast into the arena at a gallop. As in racing, the horse circles to the left (counter-clockwise).

Always subject to improvement, Riata's system has grown beyond tradition in a number of ways. "Usually trick-riders take their horses about a quarter of the way up the arena and face them into the center, then they peel off and go around from there," says Jennifer. "We did that when we started, because we were told that was what we were supposed to do, but we found that the horses got antsy being out in the open arena. And in that position, when you're getting ready for a trick the audience can see you. So we decided to move our station to the near end of the

Opposite: Cynthia Beltran has a perfect start as she prepares to do a Backbend. **Top right:** *Each girl waits at "the station," the starting and stopping point at one end of the arena, until Tom cues her to begin her routine.* **Bottom right:** *Tom intently watches Cynthia executing a Stroud Layout and prepares to send the next girl out at the proper time.*

> ## *"I carry Riata with me always in my heart, mind, and soul."*
>
> — Joanna Herrera-Howard
> Riata girl 1978–1994

arena where the horses could face into a fence, almost like being in a stall or a corral with the other horses. Standing together like that gives them herd security so they aren't as distracted by the crowd or action of the arena. Also, it's more dramatic to see a galloping horse and rider suddenly appear from one end of the arena at full speed rather than watching a horse and rider in the center prepare for the trick, then try to get up to speed."

Working with the Horse's Instincts

Okay, so your horse is running true, he's made the turn and is thundering straight and smooth along the far side of the pennant back to his buddies at the station while you still have your hands full performing tricks. This sounds like a bowling ball about to knock down all the pins! Here again, training proves critical.

"We want the horse to run all the way to the station but not plow in full-barrel, bumping other horses and stopping hard," Jennifer explains. "We train them to come in straight and stop smooth without a lot of rigamarole. Occasionally one might bump another, but not often or hard."

Most of this training is based on a horse's natural thought processes and social instincts. Since horses are flight animals from a herd society, running, returning to a band, and being mindful of the herd are all natural for them.

Performing with New Horses

Riata's improved system is especially valuable when the team must perform without their own well-trained horses. This is often the case in international venues where expense or quarantine restrictions prevent Riata's horses from being shipped in for performances. Anyone who's trained a horse knows that this is an incredible feat, especially when you consider how much a trick-rider depends on her horse's cooperation.

If luck's with them, the Cowboy Girls may find a horse or two with trick-riding experience, but most often, they must start from scratch with green horses they've never seen before. This was the case when they agreed to perform in Australia at the first-ever Equitana Asia-Pacific show in November, 1999.

"When we train foreign horses we really simplify what we ask of them," explains Jennifer. "We focus on their learning the pattern, rating, and becoming familiar with the

Left: The girls line up to pose before a performance.
Opposite: Each girl must perfect a variety of tricks to perform on unfamiliar horses while traveling in foreign countries. Different tricks suit different horses' dispositions. Here, Jennifer Welch does the Suicide Drag on Geneva.

different weight changes and odd positions trick-riding requires. Since we don't just sit on his back — suddenly we're off to the side, or standing up, or vaulting side-to-side, or hanging off his back — the horse needs a chance to adjust and accept that."

This simplified system, coupled with Riata's calming station placement, has proven successful with horses worldwide. "When we went to Equitana in Australia we had nine days to take green horses we'd never laid eyes on and train them for trick-riding in the biggest horse show in the Southern Hemisphere," says Jennifer. "You can't pull that off without some kind of a system!"

Some kind of a *Riata* system.

Riding Bareback

As horse trainer and former Riata student Liz Malloch Doe notes, "A horse is a big animal that can pack five hundred pounds per hoof. It has a heart, mind, and soul, and you have to learn to navigate it. You can't just stick a quarter in and ride. There's a lot to learning to ride."

And the best way to begin is bareback. "When I started my riding school all my students rode bareback," Tom recalls. "You know why? Well, it wasn't because I knew the value of it; back then I didn't even know what leads were. They rode bareback because I had pads and I didn't have money to buy all those saddles! I made the kids think that bareback riding was *the thing*. As it turns out, it *is* the best foundation for riding. But I discovered

Above and below: *All students must develop a secure and well-balanced seat. Cynthia Beltran here moves her arms in rhythm with the horse's stride to develop a feel for timing.*

that by accident!" Once Tom realized how effective bareback riding is in synchronizing movement and balance between horse and rider, it became the Riata Way.

THE PERFECT BALANCE

As a child learning to walk you instinctively discover where your center of gravity and balance points are. When you sit on the back of a horse, the center and balance points change, and the balancing act depends on your legs and hips. Achieving balanced equitation to control the upper body on a moving horse, without depending on the security of holding tight to the reins, is the essence of "a good seat."

Developing Your Own Instincts

"A trick-rider can't hold on to the reins; she must be free," notes Jennifer. "We're adamant about good equitation since a good seat gives balanced control, which frees the rider from the need to balance on the reins. That's why we do so many 'hands-free' arm exercises. These build confidence, a good seat, and stable balance. The rider gets in touch with the rhythm of the horse since her arms move in time with his front legs. Specifically, at the lope, when that inside left foot hits the ground, your arm movement must coordinate with it. That puts that timing into your subconscious so when you're actually trick-riding you don't need to

Jennifer Welch spots Cynthia Beltran as she executes a Shoulder Stand on the vaulting barrel, an important and well-used piece of training equipment at the ranch.

think about it, you *instinctively* move on the right beat. Once you get these important basics down, it's easy."

While a Cowboy Girl is trick-riding, her life literally hangs on the instincts and balance she develops, as this anecdote illustrates. Janna Copley recalls, "At one of our Equitana performances in Germany we were all loping around the arena doing the Hippodrome Stand, saluting and thanking the audience during the finale. I was leaning out over my horse's neck when suddenly my left foot strap gave way and flung me to the off-side of my horse. The crowd gasped as I instantly grabbed the mane, the rein, whatever I could on my way down and looped my leg around the horse's neck.

"So now I'm under the horse's neck with my leg looped around . . . it was so quick Tom didn't see what had happened, all he saw was this really dangerous situation as I came around by him. He growled, 'Get back up on your horse!' and heaved me up as we passed. My foot was still tangled in part of the strap so I couldn't swing all the way back on. I was stuck, so I held on like a monkey and rode out on the front of my horse's neck, waving to the crowd.

"If I hadn't grabbed the mane and Tom hadn't boosted me it could have been a *huge* disaster. But in all the years of being out there I've never once panicked because we're trained to respond instantly and instinctively."

*Opposite: Riata Ranch incorporates training methods used by the American Vaulting Association. Multi-Silver Level Champion Vaulter Crystal Pakizer observes as Jennifer Welch and Cynthia Beltran train on the barrel. **Right:** Jennifer and Lacey Coelho work on balance, body control, and suppleness.*

Never Give Up

As we've seen, Tom expects his girls to do well, he shows them how to do well, and then they want do well. This develops a can-do attitude that won't quit. As Kathy Copley says, "That's one of the things you learn: 'No' just doesn't exist. There's really no such thing. It's just a matter of figuring out a different way to do it until it becomes 'Yes'."

Similarly, one of Tom's signature slogans is "Begin again, don't quit." At the age of thirteen, Laurie McWilliams took that message to heart in her attempt to learn an extremely difficult trick, the Side Cartwheel. Somersaulting off the side of a galloping horse, the rider flips in the air, hits the ground, and vaults back up, landing backward on the horse's neck. In one afternoon's practice, Laurie fell *sixteen times in a row.*

Now some would have quit after the first fall; many more would have quit after the fifth fall; certainly most would have quit after ten falls in a row, but Laurie didn't. She kept on trying — not because Tom or anyone else told her to, but because she wanted to learn this trick and couldn't figure out why she wasn't getting it. Finally, too tired to continue, she quit for the day.

Still mentally searching for the missing key to success, she got her horse cleaned up and bedded down. Then an exhausted young Laurie McWilliams sat down outside the horse's stall and cried.

Normally, the Side Cartwheel is performed by men, because most women don't

Top: *Paula Herrera stretches to prepare to do a Backbend.* **Bottom:** *Tom Maier shares a story with Cynthia and Elizabeth Beltran and Jennifer Welch.* **Opposite:** *Jennifer exhibits a secure seat as she enjoys a run on Rocky.*

have enough upper body strength for the necessary lift. Ultimately, Laurie triumphed, becoming the only woman ever to master this formidable trick. Laurie succeeded only because she wouldn't let herself quit.

At Riata Ranch Tom Maier unleashes girl power, then sits back marveling at the results.

Emotional Fitness

Cool heads, calm horses, and a can-do attitude are essential in trick-riding, since anything less may spell disaster. The even, rhythmic, round-corral training at Riata allows horse and rider a focused, calm environment in which to rate themselves physically and emotionally.

However, when horse and rider appear in unfamiliar arenas with banners, laser lights, crackling loudspeakers, fanfare, flags, and fireworks, plus rodeo acts with longhorn cattle, gunfights, wild Indians, and flaming wagon trains, all surrounded by a living, breathing ocean of spectators, cool and calm can suddenly evaporate. This is when emotional fitness is vital. This is when Riata's quiet, no-nonsense, can-do attitude pays off.

With months of training and seasoning in place, horse and rider know the routine, and the rest boils down to the awareness and trust found in the psychic connection between them. The rider must be tuned in to her horse and defuse unrest before it explodes. Likewise, the horse must trust that his rider won't let him come to any harm. This is where they both "turn and face the train."

Opposite: At the end of the day, Tom Maier and Cynthia Beltran discuss goals and strategies for the next morning.
Right: *The Cowboy Girls enjoy a snack and conversation at the end of a hard-working training session.*

DAY'S END

Emotional fitness training continues after the ride, because a horse must be put away in a calm frame of mind. You do not want him fretting all night, for he may decide he won't sign on for *this* line of work anymore! Horses find comfort in calm routines. This calm overshadows any anxiety the day may have supplied.

Once the horses are settled in, evenings are a time for relaxation and reflection. Training and chores are over; the horses are bathed, doctored, watered, fed, and put away; the pasture stock are in for the night; and everyone gathers in the courtyard circle, smiling, laughing, sharing tales of the day's events and plans for tomorrow.

"Riata Ranch is a part of our hearts that will always exist."

— Joanna Herrera-Howard
Riata girl 1978–1994

Riata's courtyard offers views of every point of the Ranch: the railroad tracks, the tack room, the classroom, barn, and arena. It's all neat, tidy, and quietly released from the day's commotion. The cool six o'clock breeze kicks up, stirring the leaves to a whisper, breathing in a sense of calm with the dusk. Now you relish a feeling of total satisfaction and remember why you're here.

These quiet, golden moments are Riata at its best.

"Make a Hand"

Cowboys live by their horses, their heads, and their hands. The simple statement "He's a good hand" is a prized tribute describing the all-around cowboy. A jack of all trades and master of many, a good hand personifies the work ethic of America's West and is quick to give a hand to help out, take a hand in partnership, or shake a hand to seal a deal. This is both Tom Maier's heritage and the legacy he passes on to his Cowboy Girls, for at Riata they're bent on making good hands.

When Tom says, "Make a hand," his young charges hear, "Tough up, don't quit, work it through, you can do it!," and their resolve strengthens into determination. "Tom wouldn't have me do it if he didn't think I could," Janna Copley says confidently. Trust in their coach bolsters faith in themselves.

"Make a hand" is Riata backbone. When life deals you a tough hand, be a hand. Use your wits to figure a way to beat the odds, your strength to persevere, and your ingenuity to re-invent dreams anew.

Amanda Welty brings up the cattle for team roping. The Riata girls do all of the daily and seasonal work of the ranch and are esteemed as top hands by other area ranchers and cowboys.

The accident that crushed his knee and his hopes of a roping career showed Tom that some of life's most devastating detours turn out to be the best journeys. As every rider knows, when you're on horseback a paved road isn't necessarily the best, the quickest, or the most rewarding trail open to you. As Brenda Sampietro notes, "Tom taught us integrity, perseverance, and to accept and love one another. If it wasn't for that accident that made him take that first student, none of us would have had this wonderful foundation."

The Changing Faces of Riata

One of Tom's most valuable attributes is a positive, resourceful, and enterprising approach to life. This is the core of the Riata program: Always look ahead, define what's best, re-position yourself as needed, and set goals to realize your vision. Reflecting that spirit, the Riata Ranch program has evolved through many reincarnations from riding academy to summer camp, show barn, Mexican Review, Roping Stars, Cowboy Band, and now the Riata Ranch Cowboy Girls. Like a fabulously sequined snake Riata keeps shedding its old skin, each time unveiling a more amazing and beguiling new hide.

Often in life individuals are faced with reinventing themselves or their careers, yet are at a loss as to how to go about it. "Get

Left: The late Montie Montana, shown here performing for a crowd at Riata Ranch in 1976, was a beloved mentor of the Cowboy Girls. They dedicated their appearance in the 2001 Tournament of Roses Parade to his memory. Opposite: From left, Laurie McWilliams, Crystal Pakizer, Idalia Reveles, Cynthia Beltran, Elizabeth Beltran, Kansas Carradine, and Jennifer Welch pose at Equitana USA in Louisville, Kentucky, in 1998.

connected to your world," states biochemist Kathy Copley, who learned personal re-invention while at Riata. "One of the great things about Tommy is he talks to everyone. He's sincerely interested in people and as a result he has friends everywhere — from field hands to celebrities. Where others may have a network of contacts in business, Tommy has a network of *friends* that he calls on, and they know they can call on him."

Learning from the Pros

This network is the foundation for the valuable mentoring that Riata enjoys. If the girls need training beyond Tom's or Riata's expertise, Tom plugs into his network and presto, there's a class in vaulting, modeling, dressage, elocution,

or costume design taught by skilled professionals. In the past, the late, legendary trick-roper Montie Montana often stopped by to give a trick-roping clinic.

"There were six of us who first learned to trick-rope from Montie Montana," Jennifer Welch recalls. "He'd brought only two ropes, so you spun until you made a mistake, then passed the rope to the next in line. In the beginning, no one stood in line very long, but the incentive was, 'Two ropes and six of us . . . if I want to learn to do this, I'd better learn to hang in with this rope as long as I can.' Pretty soon, we were standing in line for a while as each of us learned to keep it spinning. Finally, we got good enough to get our own ropes." The rest, as they say, is history.

★ Life Lessons ★

Janna Copley
(Cowboy Girl from 1968 to 1985)

"As a model I'm constantly judged by my looks. That can make some people full of self-loathing. But I know I can trick-ride, herd cattle, rope, drive a stagecoach, and make a hand. Riata Ranch gave me the inner respect most models don't have. Tom told me the contents are more important than the container. I know I will be successful at whatever I choose to do."

THE COWBOY CODE

Riata Ranch gives its students a solid foundation rooted in traditional cowboy values. Having grown up in a time and place that were still governed by traditional values and the Code of the West, Tom has planted those values deep in Riata Ranch. Cowboy values have served Tom and Riata well over the years, passing on ideals such as living your word, doing your job well, honoring your commitments, and treating others fairly. "Living by your conscience" is the best summary of the Code of the West. It is a strong notion, but one that makes it crystal-clear that at Riata everyone is accountable for her own choices and actions. This pretty well eliminates excuses.

No Excuses and No Complaints

As the record shows, even during numerous life-threatening illnesses and accidents Tom has been the proverbial rock, showing courageous calm and logical realism rather than railing against fate. In entertainment his business may be drama, but in an emergency he's all business and no drama at all.

This is the example he sets for Riata: Assess the situation, do whatever possible to improve it, then accept the outcome. When the outcome is arduous he acknowledges, "This too shall pass." When the outcome is favorable he notes, "Things usually work out for the best." Either way, he accepts life in stride.

Left: *Idalia Reveles and Cynthia Beltran work the cattle chutes.* **Opposite:** *Jennifer Welch and Idalia ride across a meadow.*

"Growing up, I was always in the hands of people my grandfather's age," notes Tom. "Older men who took time to teach me the ways of the West, like Ky Wilhoit and Mickey Millrick . . . real cowboys who lived by their word and the Code. You see, the Code of the West *made* you what you were; you'd better live by it or you wouldn't survive.

"It's not that way anymore. We're living in another time. I don't think I think different, but I guess growing up with the Code gives me different expectations than people nowadays. Sometimes I have a difficult time in today's world not to betray myself, but Riata Ranch is my own society based on the Code and I still live by it today."

A CROWN OF DISTINCTION

The cowboy hat is a potent symbol of cowboy values. As Tom notes, "There are few items in the history of American culture that carry the same iconic weight as a cowboy hat. It is one item of apparel that when worn in any corner of the world receives immediate recognition.

"The cowboy hat is not a very old invention, dating only from 1865 when John B. Stetson produced the first, but our language is peppered with 'hat talk.' To keep a secret, you 'keep it under your hat.' To make a collection, you 'pass the hat.' When you take a chance, you 'bet your hat.' To compliment a

Opposite: Lacey Coelho looks up through a sea of cowboy hats. Right: Tom Maier has a special way of shaping a cowboy hat to make it look and feel right. And hats, he says, should always rest on their crowns, not on their brims.

hero you say, 'I take my hat off to you.' To celebrate, you 'throw your hat in the air.' Only when you're absolutely sure of the result do you risk claiming, 'I'll bet my hat.' You should be prepared for anything 'at the drop of a hat.' To compete, you 'throw your hat in the ring,' but people who don't know what they're talking about are 'talking through their hat.' You know you're at a friend's house when he says, 'Set your hat anywhere.' And, of course, everyone knows," Tom says with a smile, "only good guys wear white hats.

"There's also a course of etiquette surrounding a cowboy hat," Tom continues. "A gentleman always removes his hat when he first meets a lady, then on subsequent meetings, he tips his hat to her. It's polite to remove your hat when you enter a home, but you should never set a hat on its brim, always on its crown . . . and it's considered bad luck to place your hat on the bed.

"You can tell a lot about a person just by looking at their hat because real hands take pride in shaping their hat to fit their personality, their work, and even the area of the country that they're from.

"So a cowboy hat's much more than headgear: It's a national icon as universally recognized as the American flag or the Statue of Liberty. It commands respect and should be treated with respect, which is why each and every Riata Girl wears her hat as a crown of distinction."

Left: *A Cowboy Girl isn't complete without her hat. Here, Kansas Carradine and her horse explore the high country.*
Opposite: *Riata girls get ready for action, adjusting their hats, because real cowboys never lose their hats. From left, Paula Herrera, Cynthia Beltran, Idalia Reveles, and Jennifer Welch.*

"Make a Hand"

COWBOY PAYCHECKS

Since their vocation is their namesake, cowboys wear their work as proudly as they wear their hats. This is one job whose worth is measured by the man, not his bank account. For most cowboys, the ability to live and work the life they love counts more than a bulging bankroll. True to that tradition, Tom has never accumulated much money, even with all his professional achievements and Riata's amazing successes. In the real treasures of life, however — friends, family, character, respect, and grand experience — he's richer than Rockefeller. Money's just not what it's about for Sundown Tom. He's fully satisfied with the cowboy paychecks of confidence, accomplishment, and respect earned through his life's work. That example is perhaps Tom's greatest gift to all who cross the tracks to enter Riata Ranch.

Rich in Respect

"Tommy hasn't gotten rich doing what he's doing," observes rodeo producer Cotton Rosser, "but he's got ten million dollars worth of friends. Because of lack of financing he can't spend a lot on horses, so we used to give him horses to use at times. Tommy and those girls can take any kind of a horse and make it usable. Once we took a bunch of bronc colts up there. Those girls got on those colts and rode! Tom said, 'If you get bucked off, just get right back on and go again.' That was the wildest bit of cowboying I ever saw!"

Opposite: Lacey Coelho and Amanda Welty practice team roping. Top right: Riata girls bring in a mixed herd of steers, longhorns, and buffalo. Bottom right: Jennifer Welch approaches an unbroken mustang.

> ## "A Cowboy Girl knows where to be, when to be, how to be, why to be . . . and what to do when she gets there."
>
> — Tom Maier

Following in those footsteps, every Cowboy Girl not only wears the Rafter-Double-R brand, but she *rides for the brand,* demonstrating Riata values. She has practiced and prepared for all sorts of work and competition. In addition to learning exacting trick-roping and perilous trick-riding, the Cowboy Girls have been trained in all types of ranch skills from colt starting to cow-horse reining, from team roping to cutting cattle, along with driving stagecoaches and most everything in between.

Cowboy Pleasures

Janna Copley recalls some of her favorite memories as a Riata Ranch hand: "Carrying a newborn calf over the saddle of my horse on a cattle drive. Such a little, precious life. And the time Tom's buffalo, Dakota, got out and we had to go find him, rope him, and bring him back. That was random even for Riata!"

This was proven in the very heart of cowboy country when Riata participated in the July 2000 Wild West Fest in Telluride, Colorado. Cowboy Girl Kansas Carradine entered the hotly contested Celebrity Cutting Competition hosted by six-time World Champion Rodeo Cowboy, Larry Mahan, and won handily.

Top: Kansas Carradine competes at the 2000 Wild West Fest Celebrity Cutting Competition. Bottom: Larry Mahan interviews the winner.

READING HORSES AND PEOPLE

A defining quality of master horsemen is the ability to "read" a horse — to instinctively divine his character and capabilities. Tom is a master at reading both horses and people. One of his most effective traits is that he respects children and pays attention to each one's unique character. He studies a youngster the way a diamond cutter assesses a raw stone. Then he cultivates the gem inside until its natural, inner fire outshines the competition.

Through his programs, Tom helps identify and nurture each student's individual strengths and shows how to turn perceived weakness into advantage. At the age of ten, Cynthia Beltran's precocious talent so reminded Tom of golfer Tiger Woods' youthful excellence that he nicknamed her Tiger. When she voiced concern that people didn't respect her because of her diminutive size, Tom reassured her. "People do favor you because you are petite," he said, "but you win their respect when you show them in spite of your size you're no weak little kitten — you're a trick-riding, trick-roping *tiger!*"

A Tribute to Tiger

Recently Tiger received the following hand-written note: "I am so proud of you and your work with Riata Ranch. It is a thrill to have a student involved in such a well-known and interesting program. I am also impressed with your work at school and

Tom poses with a future Cowboy Girl, Rosita Beltran, the younger sister of Cynthia and Elizabeth.

good citizenship! Your principal, Ms. Ahlstrand." Now how often does a principal take the time to personally commend a student in this manner? That spells respect.

"Tommy is really a different sort of cat and he's been wonderful for the horse industry," says Cotton Rosser. "As the saying goes, 'The outside of a horse is good for the inside of a person.' I think you can say the same about Tommy Maier. If you send your chil-

dren to him, he respects them and teaches them horsemanship and roping and all those things, but he also teaches them to be wonderful young ladies. He instills showmanship and manners, and because of his teaching they're really an elegant bunch of girls. As many students as he's had, he's never had any problems with them, and a lot of them have gone on to be very, very successful people. That's a real tribute to him."

THE IDEAL HORSE

In selecting horses Tom assesses strengths and weaknesses just as he does with people. "When I look for a trick-riding horse I want a sound eight-year-old that's lived a little and learned a lot," says Tom. "We don't fool with colts because their inexperience could ruin us. You need an adult that's lived some and accepts what you want of him.

"For our program with young girls, we like a horse standing between 14 and 15 hands high, with good conformation, sound mind, and defined withers so the saddle sits well. A trick horse must also have heart and staying power so it won't give up. The memorable ones are usually streetwise extroverts that have a bit of *sting* to them — they're *horses,* not pets. You can see they have a different look in their eyes and ears; they're anything but ordinary.

"Then we build a bond with that horse. They need to trust us because we do everything on them, under them, all around them. They must trust and respect us and we must trust and respect them. That's important!"

Iron Eyes

One particularly memorable horse is Iron Eyes, named after Tom's friend Iron Eyes Cody, the well-known Native American actor remembered for a poignant anti-pollution campaign in which he was shown with a single tear running down his face.

*Opposite: One of Riata's most beloved horses was named after Tom Maier's friend Iron Eyes Cody. Both man and horse pose here with Tom, Janna Copley, and Mrs. Cody. **Right:** Lacey Coelho atop Iron Eyes, who is still used for daily training.*

Still going strong at twenty-six, the equine Iron Eyes was a difficult, skittish youngster with a lot of sting who ultimately became an exemplary trick-riding mount.

"Riding Iron Eyes was like being bestowed with an honor," says Jennifer. "Both of us had been around awhile, and we were like senior partners. I had finally earned the right to be his rider. This may sound somewhat dramatic, but we retired him after my three brief years with him. Having known Iron Eyes since he first came to Riata, I have a profound respect for him and what he represents as a horse. I do not give myself any credit for outstanding horsemastership abilities, because by the time I became his rider, he was twenty-one and we retired him at twenty-four and he had already been hauled a million miles. I just had to leave him alone and do my job. I trusted him. He truly is Riata's Ideal Horse."

Renny Spencer carries Old Glory on Rosser, named for rodeo producer Cotton Rosser.

IRON EYES

"According to Tom," says Laurie McWilliams, "Iron Eyes was a real cowboy's horse. He kept an eye and ear cocked on me at all times. My movement and body language became very important. I had to learn to respect and appreciate him as a cowboy's horse or we would get nowhere fast.

"We spent many grueling hours at the race track galloping around and around in the deep sand, with me running beside him, vaulting on and off. I kept him in hand trying to take the edge off his vigorous spirit. Hour after hour, day after day I exhausted myself trying to keep up with him.

"Finally I began to understand what Tom meant about Iron Eyes being a real cowboy's horse. I was wasting my time trying to take the cowboy out of a horse that was nothing but cowboy. Being a cowboy's horse was a great thing and I needed to nurture that, not sedate it, for Iron Eyes was very capable, smart, and above all, completely honest. Honesty is a quality most desired in a trick-riding horse. I just needed to show him what we expected of him and point him in the right direction.

"Up to this point, it had been a learning experience for me, not him. With my new enlightened attitude, I now realized he would be able to start learning from me. For the past twenty years, Iron Eyes has galloped his way across thousands of miles and into the lives of many girls. He will always remain, in our hearts, a true cowboy's horse."

Laurie McWilliams calls Iron Eyes the most trusted, respected, and well-rounded trick-riding horse ever to pass through Riata Ranch.

Geneva
by Paula Herrara

I was assigned to ride Geneva a year ago. I never really knew much about her until I started performing on her. There is one thing about her that makes her unique. She has moon blindness. Geneva is blind in her right eye.

This great mare is very dependable when it comes to showtime. There is no doubt in my mind that she will run true while I execute my tricks.

Tomahawk
by Cynthia "Tiger" Beltran

Tomahawk has always been my favorite horse, even before he was assigned to me. I liked him because he was fast and got a little jumpy sometimes. I like fast; it's my nature to be fast.

Now that he is my horse and has been for the past year, we have the greatest bond. Here is why. Before he was mine, he would always try to buck during trick-riding, and he really didn't like anybody messing around on him.

Now he lets me do anything on him. We both trust each other. When I ask him something, he responds truly, and I know I can trust him. That is the kind of bond that I have with him.

Rocky
by Jennifer Welch

Let me say right now that Rocky is the smartest horse I have ever been around. People constantly misjudge and misunderstand what kind of a horse he is. You have to be strong with him or he literally takes over. I really like him because he tells no lies. He can make a fool out of you or he can make you better. That is what I like. You can't be a phony and handle a horse like Rocky. Is he a challenge for me? Yes. But that is what is so great about Riata Ranch. No matter how long you have been around or how good you are, there is always a new challenge. A new opportunity to make yourself better.

Arapaho
by Kansas Carradine

Arapaho . . . even now, after having ridden him only a handful of times in the past five years, his name brings a smile to my face. I can see his alert ears and cautious eyes. I can feel his fast, smooth gait. I feel his light mouth in the reins between my fingers.

The most special thing between us is the trustful bond we developed. As he was a lead horse, I guided him through some daunting situations, but he always trusted me and ran truly. I cherished the fact that each time I rode him, whether for ten minutes or three hours, we had a very communicative conversation. We grew to trust and understand each other. And when I get on his back now, even just briefly, we pick up in the same familiar place where we left off.

FROM ROOKIES TO COWBOY GIRLS

More important than Riata's tests on the nomenclature of the horse, tack, or even equitation are the tough tests Cowboy Girls face on the road of life. Here Riata excels at producing "Road Scholars" well-versed in lessons that build character and coping skills. As one of Riata's foremost riders, Tina Dalton-Newsome, notes, "Riata Ranch is a way of life, not a recipe, and the valuable lessons I learned there I've passed on to my children."

Within the programs and without, Tom is constantly testing his students' mettle. Says Janna Copley, "I was only six when I started at Riata and was scared to death watching the older girls ride. Tom would call out 'One, two, three!' and they'd step off loping horses in an emergency dismount. That scared me so badly I convinced myself I'd never be able to do it. Sure enough, when the time came that I was advanced enough to do an emergency dismount I stood up, stepped off, and landed on my face.

"But as I got more comfortable with riding and with my horse's speed I kept practicing and finally did it. As my training progressed, one of my favorite things became to gallop my horse as fast as I could and slip my leg over the saddle. Then I'd rein back so he'd slide to a stop as I placed one foot and then the other on the ground, and I'd step off as smooth as you please. That was great!

Left: Lacey Coelho demonstrates Roman riding. **Opposite:** *Kansas Carradine performs a Backbend and Jennifer Welch does a Tail Drag on Galt.*

Turning something I was so scared of — and convinced that I could never do — into one of my all-time favorite things! That was a terrific lesson for me not to place restrictions on myself."

Riata's programs and horses are wonderful vehicles for lessons that generate personal empowerment. The horses that attract the children also teach them, turning horse-crazed rookies into strong, savvy Cowboy Girls. And as Tom notes, "It's not just horses, it's what horses do for people that's important."

Cowboy Up

Horses were instrumental in an inspired lesson that Laurie McWilliams and Janna Copley shared in 1977. "We were competing in the final Reining Cow Horse Class of the season. It was a large class for Seventeen-and-Under at the Santa Cruz County Horse Show," reports Janna. That show would turn out to be the last competition Riata girls ever entered. "Tom wasn't there due to his en-counter with cancer. He'd just told us before we left. That was the first time any of us had ever seen Tom cry. At the time he didn't know how long he had to live, and being only fourteen, Laurie and I assumed the worst. All the way to the show Laurie and I cried, talking about all the wonderful times Tom had given us. Now he'd sent us to represent Riata in this last show. This was our chance to make him proud of us. We decided to prove to Tom that we could carry on by placing first and second in that class.

"Words can't express the feelings Laurie and I had that day, but we rode into that arena two inches taller and came out two ribbons and a belt buckle greater. Riata left the world of competition with her head held high when I took first and Laurie took second. It was so great! This was for Tom and we did it!"

That triumphant show turned out to be a transition point for Riata in shifting from horse-show training to the professional trick-riding program for which it is now famous.

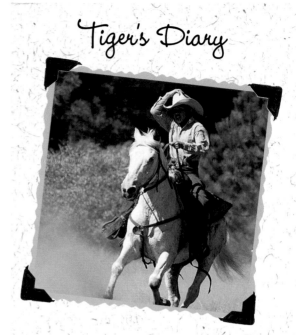

TRICKS OF THE TRADE

As with most everything at Riata, trick-riding starts from the ground up, beginning with horse care (and raking!), horsemanship skills, equitation, gymnastic training on the mini-trampoline and vaulting barrel, synchronized jogs in the round corral, and finally practicing tricks on a moving horse.

Maneuvers are categorized as strap tricks or ground tricks. Strap tricks are executed on the horse by utilizing leather anchor straps at various positions on the saddle. Stands, hangs, drags, and layouts are all strap tricks, and these tricks include such celebrated feats as the Hippodrome Stand, Fender Drag, Suicide Drag, and Tail Drag.

Ground tricks involve having to hit the ground to complete the move and require upper body strength for lift and control.

Left: *Kansas Carradine is a champion Roman Rider who has even jumped fire jumps while standing on two horses.* **Above:** *Jennifer Welch executes a Double Vault, which is a ground trick.* **Opposite:** *Kansas and Jennifer perform the Backbend and the Tail Drag, both examples of strap tricks.*

Ground tricks include a variety of vaults: Straight, Side-to-Side, and Split-the-Neck vaults, as well as High-, Double- and Reverse-Crouper Vaults and Front and Side Cartwheels. A basic Straight Vault requires the galloping rider to release her legs from the stirrups, swing over the saddle and down to hit the ground with both feet, vault herself back up, and land back in the saddle using the momentum of the horse.

Training Basics

Timing, fitness, position, and balance are the cornerstones for all tricks. Training begins with lessons on how to hold onto the horn. Hand position on the horn is critical and must be learned to the point of subconscious instinct to guard against the possibility that the wrong hand will block a move. Since trick-riding horses always track left at speed, the left hand is the anchor on the horn while the active right hand is placed on top, ready for release.

After learning hand position, a rider moves up through the strap tricks and practices the "step-through-touch" side maneuver in preparation for vaulting. Once lift and control are achieved in vaulting on both sides, a Cowboy Girl is ready to progress up through the full repertoire of more difficult vaulting tricks. As with strength exercises and trick-roping, these feats are mastered progressively to proficiency.

Specialties of the House

"Although we learn all the tricks, each of us specializes in tricks that fit the girl, depending on height, ability, and the horse," explains Paula Herrera. "It all has to come together for the performance to succeed."

Most of the Cowboy Girls are proficient in either strap or ground tricks, but some have the ability to do both well. Laurie McWilliams, for example, can do both, but her specialties are ground tricks: Side Cartwheel (she is the only woman to have mastered this), Reverse Crouper, Double Croupers, Back Bend. Jennifer Welch also can do both ground and strap tricks, but focuses more on the latter, especially the Double Vault, Split the Neck, Tail Drag, Tail Stand, One Leg Stand, and Shoulder Stand.

*Determining whether a girl is more suited for strap or ground tricks begins with identifying her abilities. **Left:** Jennifer Welch puts a young Lacey Coelho through a series of exercises. **Opposite:** Idalia Reveles is coached by veteran Laurie McWilliams in the Backbend.*

Janna Copley and Kansas Carradine are, hands down, two of Riata's best Roman Riders, says Jennifer Welch. Kansas has jumped over fire jumps and Janna has done complete reining patterns while Roman riding. Janna also has specialty strap tricks such as the Stroud Layout, Full Fender, and Hippodrome. Kansas's specialties are strap tricks, particularly the Hippodrome, One Leg Stand, and Back Bend.

The current girls are developing their own specialties. Tiger Beltran, for example, shines in the Back Bend, the Stroud Layout, and the Shoulder Stand. Paula Herrera specializes in the Parallel Fender, the Connie Griffith Drag, and the Full Fender.

"All of our girls learn to vault, and some who start with strap tricks can become proficient ground trick performers as well," explains Jennifer. "My first performance tricks were all strap tricks. Now all my tricks are ground tricks."

TEACHING EACH OTHER

At Riata Ranch, mentoring is a part of the fabric of everyday life, as it has been since the beginning, when Tom was short on staff and depended on older girls to show younger girls "the ropes." Girls teach other girls how to do tricks; they show them how to braid tails and clean saddles; they share tips on riding, grooming, and presentation; they model the best way to win over an audience. Most important are

*Opposite: "Scissors" is the name of a warm-up exercise that develops upper body strength and movement. Here, Janna Copley helps Tiger with her Reverse Scissors. **Right:** Paula Herrera receives tips from Kansas Carradine on proper balance and weight distribution for Roman Riding.*

the unspoken lessons the older, accomplished girls impart, as they demonstrate key values such as responsibility, poise, courtesy, and grace under pressure. As Tom treasures the memory of the cowboys that generously taught him his skills, the Riata girls revere the older girls who lit the way for them.

Watching the Cowboy Girls perform, it's astonishing to realize how many skills and talents are brought to bear in each thrilling presentation, and not only in staging, production, choreography, and showmanship. These girls maintain, groom, train, and haul their horses. They polish, tape, repair, and prepare tack. They design and sew their own costumes. Then they wow the crowds with their red-hot show of superb equitation, dazzling trick-roping, mind-boggling sharp shooting, and fearlessly acrobatic trick-riding. And to think all that's just in a day's work for Riata's ranch hands . . . those incredible all-around Cowboy Girls.

*Left: One of Janna Copley's specialties is the Stroud Layout, and here she helps Tiger practice this trick. **Above:** Special straps help secure feet and legs for different tricks. **Opposite:** The Cowboy Girls watch Laurie McWilliams demonstrate Around the World.*

Ride for the Brand

"*D*on't judge a book by its cover" is wise counsel, but the truth of human nature is that we are constantly judged by our appearance and actions. Particularly in professional venues, presentation counts. First impressions generate immediate interest, indifference, or dislike. For this reason, Tom Maier insists his girls always be "camera ready," presenting their best at all times, for their best is what they have to sell. In today's casually disheveled society the Cowboy Girls' confident demeanor, clean-cut appearance, and considerate manners make an impact.

Riata Ranch standards in this area are as down-to-earth demanding as Riata's work and training regimens, for here too, proven values endure. The girls are aware that they are representing the ranch at all times. Tom remembers passing through a small highway town once when he and the girls were on tour. When they entered a fast-food restaurant the waitress rolled her eyes, expecting this group of teenagers to exhibit bad manners and leave a big mess. She kept an eye on them and was pleasantly surprised by their responsible behavior. When they left, having cleaned up after themselves, the waitress called after them to compliment them.

Jennifer Welch and Kansas Carradine excel at presentation, and their joy in performing is obvious. Here they proudly salute the crowd after a performance.

Holding Your Head Up High

One important aspect of a Cowboy Girl's education echoes from an ancient, universally resented maternal supplication: "Stand up straight!" Well, much as it hurts to admit it, Mom's right. Good posture is the skeletal foundation of personal bearing, proper equitation, and lifelong fitness.

"At Riata we emphasize staying fit and strong," advises Jennifer Welch. "Don't lose your energy and your activity over the years. Many schools have dropped gym classes, and recent reports indicate obesity is becoming an epidemic in the United States. Our hope is that the fitness training each girl gets here she'll take with her. In addition to fitness we teach movement: how to walk up and down stairs gracefully, how to sit and stand properly, how to make an entrance. And, yes, we do walk around with books on our heads to keep our chin lines parallel to the ground."

Former Riata student Diana Pierce laughs as she recalls a posture lesson from Tom. "I vividly remember Tom telling me, 'Sit up straight in the saddle; don't slump over like a sack of potatoes!'

"It hadn't occurred to me that I wasn't sitting up straight, but he came over to the horse, placed his hand in the middle of my back and made me sit up straight. From that moment on I had the straightest back of any of those riders. To this day people compliment me on my posture."

Wherever they go, the Cowboy Girls' camera-ready appearance attracts attention. People can't help but notice (and often compliment) the quiet confidence and charged aura that radiate naturally from the troupe. **Left:** *(clockwise from top left) Lacey Coelho, Idalia Reveles, Tasha Candela, and Elizabeth Beltran.* **Opposite:** *(from left) Paula Herrera, Jennifer Welch, Tiger Beltran, Idalia Reveles, and Kansas Carradine.*

Paula Herrera

(Cowboy Girl from 1997 to present)

"At the age of thirteen I first set foot on the sandy grounds of Riata Ranch. I was captured by the magical, yet real world there. Over time I was able to create me, the me that I am today.

"I was faced with enormous challenges every day. At times I thought they were impossible to meet, but then I found out that I was still capable of much more.

"I'm one of the luckiest people in the world."

"Since 1983," Diana continues, "I've been a broadcaster at NBC affiliate KARE-TV Channel 11 in Minneapolis, so I have my picture taken all the time for publicity or with fans of the station. I have to credit Tom with making me aware of my presentation — what looks good and what doesn't."

Jennifer agrees. "Because of my Riata training I've had good posture from an early age and was never a kid just plopped in front of a TV," she notes. "I can't say enough about the benefits of good posture and having led a physical life, benefits I'm reaping now, more than twenty years later. And starting at Tiger's age is best. She'll have that forever."

The Look of Eagles

Proper motion supports physical health, but bearing is more than posture and a graceful carriage. As an astute horseman, Tom recognizes that champion horses not only carry themselves well, they have the "look of eagles" — that charismatic spirit of self-confident inner strength and naturally proud bearing. The programs at Riata are designed to develop the same championship poise in the Cowboy Girls. Tom knows this is the mark of a winner that discerning people recognize immediately. This is why he stresses the importance of posture, presentation, and poise . . . they add up to championship bearing.

Developing good posture is a prelude to developing a successful attitude and a positive self-image. From left, Dominique Mercado, Amanda Renstrom, Crystal Pakizer, Elizabeth Beltran, and Idalia Reveles.

Idalia Reveles

Kelly Mancha

Lacey Coelho

And that pays off in competition, it pays off in life, and it pays off when the Riata Ranch Cowboy Girls represent the United States throughout the world.

Pride + Respect = Success

Such a positive bearing translates into winning actions that are obvious to all. "Because of my work at Riata," sixteen-year-old Paula Herrera reports, "I'm more organized and self-confident. I'm not ashamed of what I look like; I accept myself and can present myself in front of people. Teachers often compliment me on things that I do differently from the other students — the way I speak to them or shake hands."

Paula's confidence reflects Tom's belief that a deep, abiding respect for others builds esteem in the students themselves and promotes regard for authority. This, coupled with their can-do attitude, puts Riata girls at the head of most any class.

Social graces, discipline, and respect are the mainstays of Riata Ranch standards at home and away. On the road, Cowboy Girls are even expected to keep their hotel rooms tidy. "Even though we rent the room for the night, it's not ours," explains Jennifer. "When you're sharing a room with others and you throw your clothes all over and are messy . . . that doesn't show much respect, and that's not the Riata Way. It's as easy to hang a shirt up as it is to throw it on the floor, and that small action shows respect for the people you're with and the establishment

Like so many others who have gone through the program before her, Paula Herrera has gained self-confidence and respect for others, the Riata Way.

"No matter where we are, we're still representing Riata Ranch."

— Jennifer Welch

you're in. I'm not saying that we're so tidy there's nothing out of place, but things are orderly and the bed's together so when the maid comes in to clean she can do her job without having to move a lot of stuff out of the way. That little discipline makes it easy and pleasant for housekeeping to work in our room, and we find they're always willing to help us with anything extra we might need because we are considerate of them.

"Obviously, behind closed doors we can let loose a little, and we do," Jennifer laughs. "But we also know how much we can't, since we're so recognizable. We're always wearing the brand, and the last thing we want is to have complaints against the Riata girls. Our philosophy is that good manners begin behind closed doors, then you take them with you into the world outside that door."

A big part of the Cowboy Girls' world outside that door is spent at school. Tom says to Paula Herrera and Idalia Reveles, "This is a new year in school, and I want you to grow from inside so that it's visible on the outside. The things you do at Riata are not easy, but because of what you do, you are a foot taller than any other girl. Now that doesn't mean you act like you're better than everybody else, but *nobody else is better than you*. What I want to see is poise that comes from the inside."

Idalia Reveles wears her cowboy hat with her own special flair.

Smile Power

One potent factor of inner poise is the simple strength of a smile. In his personal journal Tom shares his thoughts on its power: "A single smile is greater than words, for it reaches out to give a warm touch. You appear pleasant and agreeable when you smile, and it erases anger and fear. Only humans express their feelings with a smile, and for it to be effective a smile must last five seconds. The Riata girl is encouraged to smile so she can express her inner self in the public's eye. Smile at every opportunity in the next fourteen days and see the positive change that makes in your life."

THAT RIATA STYLE

In appearance and bearing there is a style, an aura, a "Riata persona" that all Cowboy Girls develop, yet Riata nurtures individuality so each girl is very much her own person. Paula Herrera's interest in presentation turned into a fascination with fashion design, inspiring her and Idalia Reveles to switch from the current baggy teenage style to wearing *dresses* at school. "These girls don't have much money, but they both sew and they make it work," says Tom. "They look nice. I am so proud of them!" Bucking the fashion trends of high school is a mark of strong individuals.

In their Riata uniform of neat jeans, pressed shirts, and white hats, Cowboy Girls may look alike to the uninitiated, but that's as far as it goes. As Idalia realized, "When I

The look of a Riata girl is unmistakable. **Left:** *Tiger Beltran poses in performance attire.* **Opposite:** *(clockwise from left) Renny Spencer, Lori Alva, and Lacey Coelho offer smiles.*

first visited Riata Ranch I noticed everyone wore cowboy hats. I'd never seen that before. Since everyone looked alike I thought everyone was the same. But when I started training at Riata, I found everyone was different. Now I know when I put on that hat, I'm an individual."

Jennifer adds, "People often think our hats are part of a costume. But they are a critical part of our everyday work clothing."

Onstage Attire

Much more than "costumes," Riata's onstage attire is specially designed to fit each performance theme. The garments are then sewn by the girls, their parents, or their friends. Through his own career and his ongoing links with Hollywood, Tom has developed a sense for bright, colorful outfits with just enough glitz to excite the eye and ignite the imagination. Having portrayed girls and women on screen, he understands how costume can help a girl create a stunning effect.

All clothing must fit properly and have the supple elasticity of a second skin, since catch points or constriction could prove disastrous. Every piece of the wardrobe is created with care, sewn with love, and worn with pride.

*Opposite: Tom Maier says there are three things you can judge a cowboy by: the way he wears his hat, the kind of boots he wears, and his belt buckle, which shows what he has achieved. All Riata girls win their buckles or the right to wear them. **Right:** The Cowboy Girls' wardrobe is designed in-house. Kansas Carradine here models several outfits; the green one is her own design.*

Tiger's Diary

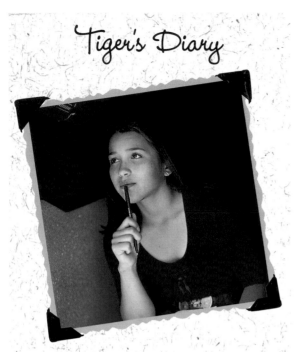

March 26

On Saturday afternoon Tom told me I was going to do a show in Norway. I didn't know where that was — I thought it was only four hours away. When my dad showed me where Norway was on the map, I was shocked. I am going to Oslo, Norway. Wow!!

Tiger

The nimble footwork of trick-riding requires sturdy shoes — a cross between a tennis shoe and ballet slipper — strong enough to withstand hitting the ground during vaulting, yet thin and smooth so feet slide in and out of stirrups and straps easily. At Riata, riders wear wrestling shoes. They are pliable so the wearer can point the toe, they give necessary ankle support, and they provide enough grip for security in the straps.

"AND SELL!"

It's hard to believe that the effervescent, attractive, confident, and articulate manager of Riata Ranch, Jennifer Welch, was ever bashful and withdrawn. The metamorphosis from a timid little girl to a vivacious, passionate professional is no less amazing than the miracle of a glorious butterfly bursting forth from its constricting chrysalis.

Above: *From left, Jennifer Welch, Kansas Carradine, Lacey Coelho, Lori Alva, and Dayleen Robison present their Spanish attire.* **Opposite:** *From left, Jennifer Welch leads Paula Herrera, Lacey Coelho, Tiger Beltran, and Idalia Reveles in practicing "And sell."*

"One rainy day when I was eleven, about twenty-five of us were at Riata and couldn't ride," Jennifer recounts. "So Tom gave us an indoor assignment, 'I want you all to write a commercial about yourself.'

"We talked about various advertisements on radio and TV, then got to writing. After we finished, some read theirs aloud, but Tom groaned, 'That's not a commercial! Re-do it so it *sells who you are.*'

"I'd patterned mine after one I'd seen on television about why I, Jennifer Welch, was the best at what I did. Since I was so shy, it sounded impossibly egotistical, but I did it."

Later, Tom put Jennifer in the Cowboy Girls band. "Now that was one of the best things that ever happened to me," she says, "because I was pitifully shy and *really* insecure about getting up in front of an audience. I could trick-ride in front of hundreds, but that wasn't scary like being up on stage. I'd never been on stage before, I'd never sung harmony, but I got up and did that, too. Eventually, I played harmonica and tambourine and danced, which really taught me how to present myself. I discovered I could perform and enjoy it.

The all-important phrase "And *sell!*" came later as a training cue for trick-roping. "It's one thing to do a trick," Jennifer explains, "but to *complete* the act you need to sell it and

*Top: Janna Copley shows Tiger Beltran the proper arm position for the Stroud Layout. **Bottom:** Janna and Jennifer Welch pose with Wendy, one of the original trick-riding horses. **Opposite:** From left, Kansas Carradine, Lori Alva, Landon Spencer, Lacey Coelho, Renny Spencer, and Jennifer perform at the California Rodeo, one of eight consecutive appearances.*

yourself to the audience. That's as important as the skill. So often, the girls would do their trick and stop short of that all-important finish. The cue 'And *sell!*' prompts them to go on, don't quit, you're not done.

"When I tell them, 'You can execute a trick, or you can perform it — you choose,' you should see the quizzical looks I get! You've shown that you can do it, now *perform* it with style, confidence, and the energy to sell it to the audience. Watching someone trick-rope is fun, but watching a trick-roping *performance* is much more exciting!"

Another thing Jennifer impresses on the girls is that when they are on stage they must perform, even when they're not center stage. "You need to be 'on' every nano-second you're in front of that audience," she says. "Keep the energy up, don't let go. These are fine points that can't really be taught because people have to want to perform in order to succeed. All I can do is consciously put in their minds, 'And *sell!*' until one day it becomes a silent cue that ignites an inner passion. That's what happened to me. It was all inside me . . . thankfully I discovered that at Riata."

Opposite and above: *The girls ride in a parade for the Wild West Fest in Telluride, Colorado.* **Right:** *Riata Ranch encourages mentoring on all levels and for all people. Jennifer Welch here mentors a child with special needs at a recent show.*

LEARNING SHOWMANSHIP

Showmanship is an ability that some people are born with and others develop only after much practice. At Riata Ranch, the older girls model showmanship for the younger ones, setting a standard of poised, smiling confidence that serves them as well in life as it does in the arena.

First Performance

Once a team member has the training, talent, attire, and presence, she is ready to begin performing in public as a Cowboy Girl. For many, that maiden appearance is at a Riata Ranch Dinner Show before family, friends, local seniors, and busloads of tourists. Organized in conjunction with the Exeter Chamber of Commerce, these informal shows are great "dress rehearsals" for introducing new tricks, staging different acts, and testing new Cowboy Girls for national tours. Served up with tasty Riata Ranch Barbecue, dinner shows have proven to be a unique and memorable draw for tourists, a delight for seniors, a convenient venue for family and friends, and a comfortable proving ground for the initiation of new Cowboy Girls. This is where Riata's show business mantle is passed on and where the girls discover the meaning behind the phrase "the show must go on."

Left: *Riding Galt, one of Riata's outstanding horses, Kansas Carradine and Jennifer Welch perform their signature combination trick saluting the United States.* **Opposite:** *Tiger Beltran is the star attraction during a parade at the Wild West Fest in Telluride, Colorado.*

ABOVE AND BEYOND

"From raking all the way up to performing, almost everything at Riata has meaning," says Jennifer. "Tom makes things special for whoever is there. I believe that's why the Riata experience is so profound for so many — there's significance in it." When what you're doing is meaningful, you become important; and if you believe in your own value, everything you do takes on meaning. And since performing to your best is Riata's highest goal, some amazing situations result when Cowboy Girls perform above and beyond.

Tough Up

"In 1977, when I was fourteen, we were performing for Chrysler Corporation at their national convention in Reno, Nevada," recalls Jennifer. "During the day we put on a trick-riding rodeo show and in the evening, we'd go to Harrah's and do a musical stage show.

"The footing in one corner of the rodeo arena was a little boggy. During the introduction ride my horse slipped and I went down with him, landing on my shoulder. I got up, and not thinking anything was really wrong, did a cartwheel and waved at the audience to let them know I was fine, then ran back to get on my horse.

Opposite: The Cowboy Girls salute the crowd at the end of a performance in Colima, Mexico.
Above: Tom Maier and the girls are focused and absorbed as they wait backstage.

"When I reached up with my left arm to grab the horn," Jennifer continues, "the most excruciating pain I'd ever experienced in my entire life shot through me, literally head to toe. That's when I knew something was terribly wrong. It was so painful I guess I went into shock and just continued on with the routine.

"Tom didn't know anything was wrong, and I didn't say anything because at that age I was really, really shy, and to call attention to myself in any way would have been a lot for me. So I went ahead and trick-rode doing the Parallel Fender, the One-Leg Stand, and the Shoulder Stand! Being in shock I wasn't feeling pain unless my arm was raised high above my head."

After the show was over, she couldn't take off her outfit or unsaddle her horse without help. "That's when I started to cry," she says, "more out of frustration than pain or fear. Tom came over, took one look, saw my collarbone was broken in half and got me to the emergency room.

"When I called my mom to tell her, she had the best attitude. Being far away from home and this being my first major accident . . . one of the most comforting things was to have my mother not be hysterical. When I heard her voice and she was okay with it, I was okay. She let me stay on. Mom and Dad have always been terrifically supportive, and I will never forget that."

Red Badge of Courage

Another example of Riata resolve occurred when the Cowboy Girls were performing at

Renny Spencer carries the Mexican flag in Colima, Mexico.

the exciting new international venue, Equitana Asia-Pacific, in Sydney, Australia, in 1999. During the main performance, Kansas Carradine was doing a Backbend when her horse suddenly changed leads behind, smashing the cantle of the saddle into her face and breaking her nose. Reeling from the impact, Kansas nonetheless held on, completing the trick although blood was flowing. "That Backbend was my next-to-last trick," she recalls. "I was okay; it didn't really hurt.

"For the final trick, I was to carry the American and Australian flags in a Liberty Stand. The funny thing was no one realized I'd broken my nose because I had a flag in each hand and the audience couldn't see my face. But blood was streaming down my face and throat, all over one of the flags, all over the saddle, all over my horse. As soon as we rode out of the arena, I jumped off and ran to the bathroom. Everyone thought, 'Whoa, she is certainly in a hurry!'

"When I came out," Kansas continues, "they saw all the blood on my outfit and Tom came running, saying, 'What happened? I didn't know you got hurt!'

"Tom's kept the flag with all the blood on it." A true red badge of courage!

Bionic Mettle

"We trick-rode on AstroTurf for the first time at the Los Angeles Coliseum in 1982," relates Laurie McWilliams. "My horse ran fine and my first trick was the Side Cartwheel where I go off the side, do a back somersault, and vault up onto the neck backward. When

Jennifer Welch greets the crowd in Colima, Mexico.

I hit the AstroTurf, my shoe grabbed instead of turning as usual and snapped my ankle. Well, that hurt!

"I probably should have pulled myself out but I didn't realize how serious the injury was. I still had Reverse Croupers and a Backbend to do and for some reason I just felt like I needed to do it . . . to finish. When

Opposite: Kelly Mancha watches the girls warm up in Telluride, Colorado. Below: From left, Tiger Beltran, Kelly Mancha, Paula Herrera, Jennifer Welch, and Idalia Reveles share a reflective moment at ringside.

the show's going fast, adrenaline's flowing and you don't realize how much you hurt at the time — you just go on and do it. So I went ahead, did my Reverse Croupers, hitting the ground two or three more times. When I came into the station tears were streaming down my face. Tom said, 'What's wrong? What's wrong?'

"'I don't know. I hurt my ankle on my cartwheel.'

"He said, 'Do you want to pull out? You should pull out!'

"Now I see life very differently than I did before Riata."

— Idalia Reveles
Riata girl 1993–present

"'No, no, no . . .'

"Here he was telling me to pull out and I still wanted to finish. 'All I have left is the Backbend,' I said. 'I can do that, I won't have to hit the ground any more.'

"So I went out, did the Backbend, and finished the show . . . on a broken ankle."

All sinew, muscle, and bone, the Cowboy Girls' lithe, acrobats' bodies are strong, yet their resolve is even stronger. It's as if these exceptional young women were assembled at Riata from a kit of titanium and steel — Bionic Cowboy Girls!

LIFE'S TAPESTRY

By working and training the right way — the Riata Way — a student gains the *security* of performing in the safest, most effective manner; the *success* of consistently replicating excellent results; and the *ability to teach* that excellence to others. And there is yet another, more personally valuable benefit in the Riata Way of training and living. Riata girls learn to sell more than a rope trick, they learn to sell their dreams and their abilities. This is a valuable asset when it comes to marketing yourself and your passion in life. This will help Paula Herrera to pursue a career in art and fashion design. It will help Idalia Reveles realize her goal to earn college money through airline service, and Tiger will rely on this ability to fulfill her dream of becoming a police officer.

Add to this high personal standards, proud bearing, self-respect, discipline, showmanship, talent, and toughness, and you have an impressive personal commodity to market in your chosen field and throughout your life. As veteran rodeo announcer Bob Tallman observed after working with Tom and the Cowboy Girls, "Riata gives young people a survival system for their adult lives."

For woven within all these Riata disciplines are the gold and platinum threads of human values and work ethics that create individual strength and character: responsibility, competence, community, dependability, accountability, competitive spirit, focus, teamwork, mentorship, personal pride, and self-esteem.

"I am the youngest of thirteen children, and my family moved to California from Mexico nine years ago when I was seven," reports Idalia Reveles. "Before I started at the Ranch you could say I was an air-head. I think most teens go through that stage. But I thank Riata very much for the lessons that we learn of life, the people that we meet, and the places that we go because it has changed my life completely. Before Riata I didn't plan ahead, I was not organized — I would just live day by day. But now I have a plan, I know what I want to do a week from now, I know what I want to do two years from now. I'm very excited because I can picture many wonderful possibilities coming up soon."

Riata's programs enable each Cowboy Girl to weave the fabric of her own life with those precious, durable strands of character, making each unique tapestry a fascinating, scintillating work of art admired by all. Whether rodeo queen or fashion model, news anchor or doctor, horse trainer or flight attendant, artist or police officer, a Riata girl's life becomes her own masterpiece, enhanced by her confident bearing, considerate actions, attractive attire, and passionate substance. This is what each Cowboy Girl learns to develop in her daily life.

Left: Riata has made Tiger Beltran proud and confident.
Opposite: Tom Maier and the girls pause for a group portrait. From left, Paula Herrera, Amanda Renstrom, Jennifer Welch, Tom Maier with Tiger on his lap, Lacey Coelho, Kelly Mancha, Tasha Candella, and Idalia Reveles.

Showtime!

The blue commercial pick-up and gooseneck trailer pull off the highway, rolling to a stop alongside the gas pumps. Instantly doors fly open and four young girls in white cowboy hats jump out. Rushing to the back, one disappears inside the trailer; two others stride to the pump, where one places the nozzle into the truck's tank and the other pulls a squeegee from the hanging wash bucket, then steps onto the bumper to scrub the wide windshield. The fourth circles the rig, checking the hitch, oil, tires, and anything else that might need attention. Meanwhile, the trailer tender makes sure all the horses are still tied safely and have easy access to feed and water. Depending on the temperature, she adjusts vents and blankets on the standing animals.

This sudden, curious "cowboy fire drill" catches the attention of other customers, who watch with growing appreciation as each girl quickly completes her task and hops back in the cab. The gas is charged, and the big rig pulls back into traffic before the others have filled their tank or paid for a soda pop! The Riata Ranch Cowboy Girls are on the road with the same quiet efficiency they display at home.

Kansas Carradine prepares mentally and physically for her performance at Equitana USA in Louisville, Kentucky.

Packing Sensibly

For the Cowboy Girls, packing is common sense: Bring what you need and don't overpack. "Unless we're in a situation where a lot of different day and evening outfits are necessary, we don't need to pack a lot," states Jennifer Welch. "If we're gone for six days, three pair of jeans is plenty because they don't get dirty from a lot of chores the way they do at home. Another thing: If you don't wear it at home, you're not going to wear it on the road. And finally, since we're pretty noticeable, good grooming is very important. Not lots of make-up; just bring your good grooming habits."

Settling In away from Home

The well-being of Riata's horses is the highest priority when the girls are traveling, because of the challenge of keeping the animals calm and fit in the midst of long hauls, new surroundings, and chaotic show events. Riata's string of horses adapts pretty well simply because they are hauled and exposed to the turmoil of show business so often. When a new horse is being added to the string, they'll haul him along with the veterans to expose him to the experience of road trips: new arenas; noisy, raucous productions; and crowded venues. The aim is to foster a relaxed, positive attitude in the string, especially right before a show.

"At the bigger events where there's a lot going on, the riders are more nervous and the horses tend to get nervous," says Jennifer, "so we like to work them for about forty minutes

Everyone helps pack the trailer for a road trip, but Jennifer Welch decides how and where everything fits.

get into this kind of a mind set. I love to perform, and I want to *enjoy* performing again.' Then I concentrated on things I knew I could do. I set goals every night and made sure I reached them because it's so important to be able to walk on stage or go into the arena with an attitude of *I can do this!* rather than *I hope this goes well . . . .*

"It's vital to differentiate between those two statements," Jennifer goes on, "because when you get negative you quit thinking and give up control. You give up the will to *make it happen.* Instead you just close your eyes and *hope* it will happen. There's no control and no power in hope. You need to *know* you can do it. And, as I've discovered, that really is a matter of positive thinking."

A Can-Do Attitude

As noted earlier, Riata instills a can-do attitude in all its students. As sage twelve-year-old Tiger Beltran observes, "Most people are afraid they're going to fail. You have to have confidence in yourself and say you can do it. I always say that to myself, and I always tell Tom, 'I can do it.' You have to have attitude and want to do it, then tell yourself you can do it."

Tom seems almost to *will* his girls to heights of accomplishment through positive thinking and trust without fear of failure. Even after a twelve-year absence from trick-riding, Janna Copley retained this attitude and trust when she rejoined the Cowboy Girls for their 1997 European tour.

Opposite: Jennifer Welch outfits Samantha Mugnier, from Marseille, France. Right: Kansas Carradine prepares for a performance.

"When I was trick-riding on a regular basis, I knew I could count on my horse and I could count on my saddle," says Janna. "But coming out of retirement I was really nervous because I didn't have either of those comfort zones. Without my own gear and a regular mount, I had only myself to count on, and I was rusty! Since leaving Riata, I'd become a model and then went on to work in the movie production department of Turner Network Television.

"I am a proud Hispanic woman, and I carry Riata with me always in my heart, mind, and soul. I want to instill this pride in every young girl that I see, including my own."

— Joanna Herrera-Howard
Riata girl 1978–1994

"Trick-riding's not something you can go to the gym and do, so I'd been away from it for eons. Plus, we were using horses belonging to the Russian Cossacks. They were used to people hanging off them but we still had to train them to our style of trick-riding and to the station routine. We only had a couple of night trainings before the show. Then, at the last minute, my horse was assigned to Kansas because she needed a horse to do a Backbend on, and hers wasn't working out.

"The horse I was given had no training at all because he'd been judged the least reliable, so we'd concentrated on training the other horses. But now, all of a sudden, he's *my horse!* And since I'm the first one out, he'd have no other horses to follow, so I'd really have to let this horse know where the pattern is!

"Coming out of retirement into this situation raised my doubts and lowered my confidence, but I knew Tom wouldn't have me do it if he didn't think I could. I trusted him to make it all work, then I trusted myself — that I could do it, and *I did!*

"When we were done, I felt really, really proud. There's nothing that I can imagine

doing that would make me feel that proud and that capable. It's a great feeling that I really can't get anywhere else."

Janna came to realize once again, "When you're working so hard to achieve your best, you don't have time to imagine the worst. If Tom says you can do something, you know you can, so you just get it done and it won't even enter your mind that you can't do it."

And what of the times when Tom's not around? "We still have Riata inside of us," Tiger says confidently. "We think of the way he would want us to do things, what he would tell us, and that's the way we do it."

SUERTE!

Just before heading into the arena, every Riata Ranch Cowboy Girl connects with her teammates by looking each in the eye, exchanging firm handshakes, and wishing one another *"Suerte,"* Spanish shorthand for "Good luck." This is a crucial part of the mental warm-up, for it bonds the troupe and bolsters individuals who may be feeling a bit overwhelmed by excitement or nerves.

When the Cowboy Girls feel a need for power beyond the realm of human mind and spirit, they find strength in Kansas Carradine's Riata Ranch Prayer: "Dear Lord, bless our horses, make them run true, and give us confidence to do a good show." Thus fortified with a positive attitude, trust in their coach,

Opposite top: Tiger Beltran says, "I'm ready. How soon do we go on?" Opposite bottom: Tom always doublechecks every saddle to make sure straps and buckles are secure. Right: Kendra Burkheimer (top) and Lacey Coelho (bottom) spend time with their horses just before the show.

confidence in themselves, and faith in God, they ride out and give their all.

And they succeed in typically dynamic Riata Ranch style, as rodeo announcer Bob Tallman notes. "I've announced thirteen-thousand performances, probably a thousand with the Cowboy Girls. Because of Riata's in-depth program the Cowboy Girls are much bigger than a rodeo show. The show is just the cake they bake, their final offering. It's exhilarating, it's memorable, it's always a positive part of every performance . . . it's everything you'd want for entertainment value."

Once in the station the girls' attention is set on Tom, who cues the critical timing of the performance. As each girl is introduced, the Cowboy Girls race around the arena.

All the World's a Stage

Fans love the speed, the spirit, the glitz and glamour of these girls on their flashy mounts. "They called us 'Ninjas on horse-back' when we toured Japan in 1981," Janna Copley grins. Nimble, athletic warriors, Ninjas are said to appear as if by magic.

"Back then," she says, "the Japanese didn't even consider women self-sufficient. Yet here we were, just young girls, doing all these dare-devil stunts and being compared to legendary warriors! We were presented to the prince, and I'll never forget the look on his face as I shook his hand. It was real admiration. He later became Japan's emperor."

Left: Janna Copley performs the Hippodrome Stand during the Cowboy Girls' 1981 tour of Japan. Opposite: Lori Alva, Landon Spencer, Lacey Coelho, Renny Spencer, and Kansas Carradine give a final salute after a performance.

Laurie McWilliams recalls other exciting venues. "Our performances in Europe are the most memorable for me, especially Equitana in Germany where so many countries participate. It's impressive just to be there. Europeans love the American cowboy, and they have nothing like our show. It's exciting, it's cowboy, it's fast-paced, and much different from dressage or jumping, which are absolutely wonderful to watch, but much slower. Since our show is so unique, we are considered celebrities.

"Audience reaction makes a performance great. When we're doing well and the crowd's with us, every trick gets better and better. We get a lot of respect from all kinds of people we look up to. Olympic riders think we're wonderful! It's really exciting to be in a foreign country, doing well, and to be so appreciated — you feel elated!"

But that respect was hard earned. "When we were representing the United States at Equitana in Germany in 1981, there was a joint press conference during which the French military did not want to be associated with us because they thought we were just 'Cowboys and Indians' and didn't have appropriate horsemanship skills," recalls Janna Copley. "After they saw us perform they came over and told us what great horsemen we were and asked if we would take a picture with them. That made us feel really good.

"Later, there was a gathering of all the nations, and they asked us to sing. We sang

*Left: Paula Herrera helps Tiger Beltran with entries in her diary. **Opposite:** Kansas Carradine, Tiger, Jennifer Welch, and Laurie McWilliams pose after a show at Churchill Downs. Riata girls have performed three times at this famous racetrack.*

'All the Gold in California' and everyone started clapping and singing along. At the end they gave us a standing ovation. I'll never forget that because it was a time when all the countries came together and pulled together in a very positive moment. Rarely do you see or feel that, and to have been a part of it was wonderful."

IT'S SHOWTIME!

The day of an event is an emotional roller coaster with the slow-building intensity of preparations: horses, tack, wardrobe, make-up, warm-up; the last-minute excitement of mounting up and pre-show parades; the nervous anticipation of waiting to go on; the nagging anxieties that creep into your mind regardless of how many great runs you've had. Then, with almost surreal suddenness, you're poised at the top, ready to take the plunge . . . Tom cues you . . . you're on!

Your horse explodes into the arena. Adrenaline pumps through your body, instantly synchronizing your heart, head, and lungs with your horse's thrusting piston rhythm. You're both on auto-pilot as practiced instinct takes over. He runs straight and true while you leap off to the right, touch down, bounce back up, spin around the saddle horn, and repeat the same fluid vault on the left side before your racing horse reaches the end of the pennant.

Rushing wind whips your hair back and

*Opposite: At the California Rodeo in Salinas, Kansas Carradine listens to some last-minute advice from Tom Maier at "the station." **Right:** The Cowboy Girls make a grand entrance at the Wild West Fest in Telluride, Colorado.*

Idalia Reveles

(Cowboy Girl from 1994 to present)

"When I'm performing, I smile from happiness. You know all those people are clapping for you and cheering you on because you are doing something that everybody recognizes all over the world.

"It's a special feeling, and my heart just wants to burst out of happiness! Performing is one of the greatest experiences in the world. I know how very lucky I am."

fills your ears with the ecstatic sounds of an astonished crowd as your mount banks the turn, heading home. Momentum and lift suspend gravity; you feel weightless as your body flies around the speeding animal. Your right leg swings over the cantle, and your left reverses in its stirrup, tucking up under the fender as you hang suspended next to pounding hooves in a picture-perfect Full Fender Drag. You pull yourself back into the saddle just in time to salute the fans smartly before your horse settles into a tight, smooth landing at the station.

Your heart soars. Nothing else gives you such a life-rush, you can't stop grinning.

"Live performance is just the best," affirms Jennifer. "There's no better emotional high you can have than live performance."

Above: The Riata girls head toward the arena to perform a trick-roping routine in Salinas, California. *Opposite:* Laurie McWilliams, Jennifer Welch, Idalia Reveles, Tiger, announcer Eddie Kutz, Crystal Pakizer, Kansas Carradine, and Elizabeth Beltran pose at Equitana USA in Louisville, Kentucky.

GRIT AND GLORY

"At one of our performances, " says Idalia Reveles, "there was a group of Japanese tourists, and every time we made a trick-riding run they would cheer us on. Afterwards they all came to us wanting to take pictures and give us little symbols from Japan for good luck. They had never seen anything like what we do. They said they would always remember us. I will always remember them."

*Opposite: Jennifer Welch shows her pride in being American, in Ridgeway, Colorado. **Below:** Tom Maier and the girls (from left, Landon Spencer, Lori Alva, Renny Spencer,nd Jennifer) relax between performances in Mexico.*

"Every audience we've had has enjoyed our show because it's so unique and different," adds Tiger Beltran. "They start screaming and shouting. The more they cheer the more we love it. I have a burning sensation of excitement inside of me to go out and perform. I want to get out there, have fun, and make the people happy. The more they cheer me on, the more I want to do it again."

In October 1999, the Cowboy Girls were invited to Oklahoma City's National Cowboy Hall of Fame to perform at ceremonies held to honor inductees who have contributed to the rodeo world. "We did a routine called 'Cowboy Heroes' as a tribute to all past trick-roping legends like Will Rogers, Gene McLaughlin, Rex Rossi, J. W. Stoker, and Montie Montana," Paula Herrera reports. "They were our mentors, and we were very proud to represent them before their families and the rodeo community. We received a standing ovation from all who were there. Afterward we were told that in all the years of performances at that event, we were the first ever to receive a standing ovation! That's incredible because as Jennifer told us, 'These people are the best or have seen the best.'

"For me performing is success," Paula continues. "You know other people have done each trick, but when you do it, it feels like the first time anyone has done it. You feel proud. It's a glory!"

From all reports, it's apparent that the real luck of the Cowboy Girls is having the experience of Riata Ranch itself: learning its lessons, gaining its strength, internalizing its resolve, honoring its heritage, reaping its rewards, and living its wisdom. As Jennifer's discovered, "Riata Ranch is not just a patch of ground, it's much more. It's an attitude we take with us, an attitude of honest pride and discipline. We show the world our best everywhere, not just when the spotlights are on us."

Tom adds, "Riata students never leave Riata. They take it with them and cherish it because this is where they found themselves."

"When I think of what I would be doing right now without Riata," says Tiger Beltran, "I thank God for having Tom. Without Tom there wouldn't be a Riata and without Riata I wouldn't be who I am right now. Before Riata I couldn't even speak up to tell people my name. Now I'm president of my school. I meet lots of people; I've been on TV; I've traveled to Norway, Australia, and quite a few states that I would never have been to without Riata. I think I was meant to come to Riata."

As Tiger's success shows, more than all the awesome talent and entertainment Riata produces, the invaluable legacy of Riata Ranch is the priceless personal gifts of direction, discipline, confidence, resolve, respect, and love that Tom and Riata selflessly pass on. These are the life-strengthening rewards every Riata Ranch graduate enjoys — genuine cowboy grit, guts, and glory.

Left: *Tiger shares a private moment with Rocky.*
Opposite: *The Riata Ranch Cowboy Girls proudly carry Old Glory in the Grand Finale at the world-famous Churchill Downs racetrack.*

GLOSSARY

Around the World. A rope trick created by the Riata Ranch Cowboy Girls in which the roper spins a Wedding Ring, maneuvers to a horizontal position, balances on one arm, pivots like a top, and returns to starting position. Shown on pages 17, 48 (top), and 97.

Backbend. A trick created by Nancy Bragg, National Cowboy Hall Of Fame inductee and famed trick rider. Using the hippodrome strap and crouper handles, the rider holds a backbend position on top of a galloping horse. Shown on pages 53, 56, 89, 91, and 93.

Butterfly. A rope trick in which the rope is spun vertically, continuously changing directions from side to side, looking like the wings of a butterfly. Basic Butterflies can be spun in front of or to the side of the roper.

Crouper handles. Special hand holds attached to the back jockey of the saddle which are used to perform all crouper tricks, the Backbend, and a variety of other tricks. Riata Ranch has all crouper handles specially made to give them proper shape and body.

Double Vault. A continuous vault from one side of the horse to the other. Shown on page 90. Also known as a Side-to-Side Vault.

Fenders. The front flaps of a Western saddle, on either side of the horn.

Front Cartwheel. A trick in which the rider stands in the saddle facing forward with both hands on the horn, somersaults off the horse's shoulder, vaults back up, and lands sitting in the saddle facing forward.

Ground tricks. Tricks in which the rider has to hit the ground to complete the move. These require upper body strength for lift and control. Ground tricks include a variety of vaults.

Hippodrome Stand. A trick in which the rider stands freely on a moving horse with both feet secured in the hippodrome strap.

Hippodrome strap. Leather strap that goes across the front of the saddle and is laced on each side to "D" rings. Used for the Hippodrome Stand, One-Leg Stand, and Backbend.

Liberty Stand. A Hippodrome Stand with the rider carrying a flag. Shown on pages 116 and 120.

Lift. Upward momentum created by the forward movement of the horse and the vaulting action of the rider. Lift is necessary when doing any type of ground trick.

Longe line. A long rope attached to a horse's halter or bridle while the horse works in a circle at a set distance from the handler. Longe lines are used in vaulting, but not in trick-riding. They are never used at Riata Ranch.

Ocean Waves. A variation of the Butterfly rope trick in which the roper keeps a vertical loop circling continuously around the roper's body creating a wavelike effect.

Parallel Fender. A trick-riding routine in which the rider bends the knee under the fender of the saddle and then twists it backward to create support for the body while the left hand holds the horn. The body is parallel to the horse with the rider's head and shoulders facing the same direction as the horse's.

Rating. A term describing a horse's ability to maintain a consistent pace and a calm demeanor at every speed, without direction from his rider.

Remuda. A herd or string of saddle horses.

Reverse Crouper. A trick in which the rider starts sitting on the rump of the horse facing forward, vaults to the ground, flips, and lands in the saddle facing backward, using the crouper handles.

Riata. Spanish word for "rope."

Rollover. A variation of the Butterfly rope trick in which the rope is maneuvered to slowly roll over the roper's arm, shoulder, or head.

Roman Riding. A routine in which the rider stands freely on two moving horses without the aid of straps. Shown on pages 88, 90, and 95.

Shoulder Stand. A routine in which the rider is in an upside-down position over the left shoulder of the horse with the left hand on the horn and the right hand gripping a handle on the right side. Shown on page 61.

Side Cartwheel. Somersaulting off the side of a galloping horse, the rider flips in the air, hits the ground, and vaults back up, landing backwards on the horse's neck.

Split the Neck. A trick in which the rider vaults to the ground, flips in the air, and lands backwards on the horse's neck.

Station. The area of an arena in which the trick-riders begin and end their routines.

Straight Vault. A trick in which the rider sits in the saddle facing forward with both hands on the horn, kicks the right leg over to meet the left leg, hits the ground in time with the horse, and vaults back up, landing forward in the saddle. Also known as a Single Vault.

Strap tricks. Tricks (such as stands, hangs, drags and layouts) executed on the horse using leather anchor straps at various positions on the saddle.

Suerte. Spanish word for "luck."

Suicide Drag. The left foot is secured in a leather strap anchored on the off side. The rider falls into an upside-down position with her head and hands close to the ground, very often dragging on the arena floor. Shown on page 59.

Tail Drag. A trick in which both feet are secured in straps on the back of the saddle. The rider falls into an upside-down position off the back of the horse. Shown on pages 89 and 91.

Texas Skip. A rope trick in which the roper spins a 25-foot vertical loop and jumps through it from side to side in a continuous motion. Shown on pages 47 and 48 and on the copyright page.

Wedding Ring. A rope trick in which the roper spins a loop around herself.

INDEX

The following Cowboy Girls appear in the photographs at the beginning of this book.

Cover: Cowboy Girls (from left) Jennifer Welch, Paula Herrera, Kansas Carradine, and Cynthia Beltran thunder across a California mountain meadow.

Half-title page: Jennifer Welch and Kansas Carradine salute the crowd after a performance at the California Rodeo in Salinas.

Opposite title page: Cowboy girls (from left) Elizabeth Beltran, Jennifer Welch, Cynthia Beltran, and Kansas Carradine pause to enjoy the view while warming up for a performance in Telluride, Colorado.

Title page: Paula Herrera, Jennifer Welch, Cynthia Beltran, Idalia Reveles, and Kansas Carradine pose during a break in a performance at Telluride, Colorado.

Copyright page: Janna Copley performs the Texas Skip atop her horse.

Back-cover photos: (clockwise from top): Jennifer Welch and Kansas Carradine; a poster from Riata Ranch; bathing a horse; the Riata Ranch Cowboy Girls salute the crowd during a performance; Elizabeth Beltran prepares to mount for a training session.